# A Piece of Cake

## FUN AND EASY THEME PARTIES FOR CHILDREN

# A Piece of Cake
## FUN AND EASY THEME PARTIES FOR CHILDREN

**Gwenn Boechler**
**Shirley Charlton**
**Alice Traer Wayne**

DOUBLEDAY

New York  London  Toronto  Sydney  Auckland

Published by Doubleday, a division of Bantam Doubleday Dell Publishing Group, Inc.,
666 Fifth Avenue, New York, New York 10103

**Doubleday** and the portrayal of an anchor with a dolphin are trademarks of
Doubleday, a division of Bantam Doubleday Dell Publishing Group, Inc.

Library of Congress Cataloging-in-Publication Data
Boechler, Gwenn.
    A piece of cake: fun and easy theme parties for children / Gwenn
Boechler, Shirley Charlton, Alice Traer Wayne. — 1st Am. ed.
        p.      cm.
    ISBN 0-385-24974-8 (pbk.):
    1. Children's parties.    I. Charlton, Shirley.    II. Wayne, Alice
Traer.    III. Title.
GV1205.B6 1989
    793.2′1—dc19              88-25769
                              CIP

First published in Canada by McGraw-Hill Ryerson Limited, 1987
Copyright © 1987 by McGraw-Hill Ryerson Limited

First Edition in the United States of America, 1989

To our husbands, Paul, Peter, and Mark; our children, Alitta, David, Laura, and baby W; and our future children.

# CONTENTS

# Introduction

We are three Early Childhood Education teachers with many years of experience dealing with young children and their parents. As well, we have children of our own. It is our personal experience that busy parents are searching for alternatives to expensive and commercial birthday parties. Often they are frustrated and concerned about costs, and they feel inadequately prepared to plan and host a successful party.

We believe that planning and preparing for your child's birthday party can be an enjoyable experience for you and your child. It is the purpose of this book to offer party plans and ideas on how to give an inexpensive, yet novel and fun birthday party for children under the age of 9. Included are seven birthday party themes, with easy-to-follow party plans. Each theme was chosen because of its well-known appeal to young children. We have tried out each one to make sure it goes smoothly, so you can be confident about choosing any of the themes for your own child.

Suggestions and samples of party invitations, decorations, party favors (to make or buy), games, menus, schedules, stories and thank-you notes are included in each plan. There is more than ample choice for you in every chapter. Due to the large number of ideas presented for each theme, we strongly suggest you resist trying to do all of them at your party. Remember to consider your child's age and interests, as well as what you yourself feel comfortable doing.

We suggest you plan for a party of about an hour and a half in length for children three and four years of age, and two to two and a half hours long for older children. A short party with a few well-chosen activities will be far more successful than a long drawn-out affair.

Finally, don't forget to plan for the few minutes after all the guests have left. Your child will be very excited and may feel let down when everyone is gone. Spend 10 or 15 minutes after the party quietly discussing the events of the day and the gifts received, to help your youngster come down to earth gently.

Now you're ready—be creative, enjoy, and remember: IT'S A PIECE OF CAKE!!

# Second Thoughts

• Limit your number of guests—three to eight children is a manageable group, depending on their ages.

• Prepare and set up materials before the party. When working with young children, you need to be able to change activities quickly and smoothly.

• Encourage children to try art projects on their own. Don't let them get you to do the work. Tell them to try their hardest and be sure to praise their efforts afterwards.

• Choose craft activities carefully. Some children can be easily frustrated by them.

• Supervise your party activities closely, especially when children are involved in cutting or baking activities.

• Attempt cooking activities only if you feel comfortable with them.

• Not every child likes to be "It" in a game. Many prefer to be just one of the players.

• Ask another adult to assist you with the party, if you need help.

• We strongly suggest that gifts be opened near the end of the party, to reduce the chance of loss or breakage. As well, your child may not immediately feel ready to share the new toys.

• Make a minimum of food. Children are excited and usually don't eat much. Most are looking forward to the cake and ice cream!

• Tape your party plan to the fridge or a wall for easy reference.

• Always be prepared with an extra activity in case the party goes faster than planned.

• Hold your party in a room that children can let loose in.

• Welcome your guests with a bouquet of balloons close to the entry of your home.

• Be flexible and enjoy your party!

# A Piece of Cake

# A Teddy Bear Birthday

*"Just grin and bear it"*

# A Teddy Bear Birthday

One of a child's first friends is a snuggly teddy bear or other stuffed animals. They cling to them dearly and take their teddy everywhere! Many adults still have their own teddy bears that they cherished as a child. In honor of this dear and precious friend, we planned our first party theme.

Your young guests will enjoy the many teddy bear activities—from receiving their teddy bear invitations through to munching on a teddy bear cake.

Plan a teddy bear party for young children and have fun!

## Invitations

Here are step-by-step directions for making your own teddy bear invitations. Be sure to include your child in the making of the invitations, as part of the birthday celebration.

**Materials:**
Brown construction paper
Crayons, felt pens, pastels
Scissors
Glue
Any of: wool, buttons, sequins, colored paper, cotton batten and felt. (Be creative—add what you have on hand.)

**Directions:**

1. Fold brown construction paper in half to fit teddy bear tracer (fig.12). Place teddy bear tracer on the foldline and trace pattern. Cut out traced picture, cutting through both pieces of construction paper at the same time. Do not cut across the top of the ears.

2. Decorate the invitation by adding eyes, a nose and a mouth. This can be done with crayons and felt pens, or you and your child may wish to be creative with any combination of wool, sequins, buttons and paper.

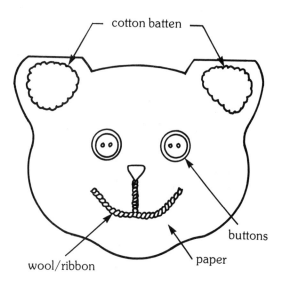

fig. 1

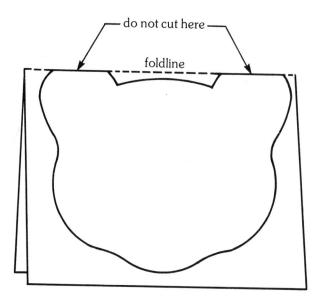

fig. 2

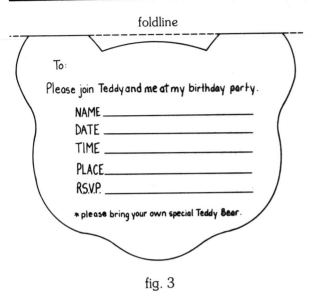

fig. 3

3. With a bold pen, clearly print all important party details inside the invitation (fig. 3).

4. Hand out your invitations a week to 10 days before the party—slightly sooner if mailing.

# Decorations

Streamers and balloons placed in the party area add a festive touch. You may wish to draw bear faces on the balloons, using felt pens, or purchase bear-shaped balloons instead. Place any of your child's extra teddy bears around the party area for decoration. Tie a big bow around each teddy bear's neck. The table may be decorated by placing a very small teddy bear in the middle for a centerpiece. White paper placemats can be custom-made using a few "store bought" bear stickers. Or you may choose to have the children decorate their own placemats as a party activity, described below.

# Party Favors

You can buy all your party favors, have the children make them all—or do a combination of both. You may even decide to make some of the favors yourself, ahead of time. Your decision should be based on the ages and interests of the children and your party budget. For younger children you will probably buy or make most of the favors, whereas older children will enjoy making them themselves. A word of caution: Be

selective, as even older children may not want to make all of the party favors described.

*Party Favors You Can Buy:*

Teddy bear-shaped ju-jubes
Teddy bear balloons
Teddy bear stickers
Teddy bear soap
Teddy bear toys (plastic bear that attaches to a pencil, barrettes with bears on them, etc.)
Teddy bear ink and ink pad, to stamp a teddy on each child's hand
Teddy bear books (see the recommended list later in this section)
Teddy bear pins

*Party Favors You Can Make:*

Be sure to have the children print their names on whatever they make.

## Teddy Bear Placemats

**Materials:**
1 white paper placemat per child
1 teddy bear placemat tracer per child (fig. 15), traced and cut out of heavy paper
Felt pens, crayons and pencils

**Directions:**
1. Give each child a placemat, a teddy bear invitation tracer and a pencil.
2. Ask children to trace one or more teddy bears onto the placemats for decoration.
3. These can then be colored with felt pens or crayons. The children may wish to add their own decorations to the placemats as well.

fig. 4

## Very Important Teddy Badges

**Materials:**
1 piece of heavy construction paper per child
1 badge tracer (fig.13) per child, traced and cut out of heavy paper
1 small safety pin each
Felt pens, crayons, pencils
Scissors
Sign with "Very Important Teddy" printed on it (fig. 5).

**Directions:**
**1.** Give each child a piece of construction paper, a badge tracer and a pencil. Have them trace and cut out their own badge.
**2.** Older children may copy the words "Very Important Teddy" from the sign onto their badge, but you will have to do this yourself for younger children.
**3.** Completed badges are then pinned on each child's teddy bear.

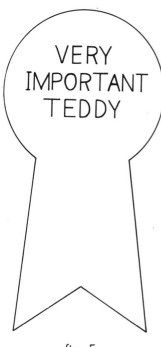

fig. 5

## Teddy Bear Party Hats

**Materials:**
1 piece of heavy construction paper per child, to fit teddy bear tracer
1 teddy bear party hat tracer (fig.14) per child, cut out of heavy paper
Felt pens, crayons, pencils
Glue
Stapler and staples
Scissors

**Directions:**
**1.** Give each child a teddy bear party hat tracer (fig.14), a piece of heavy construction paper and a pencil.
**2.** Children should then trace, cut out and decorate a teddy bear head, using felt pens.
**3.** Glue the teddy bear head on the center of the piece of long construction paper.
**4.** With the help of an adult, the children can staple the two ends of the long construction paper to make a hat that fits onto their heads. Extra construction paper may need to be cut off. See fig. 6 for a picture of the hat.

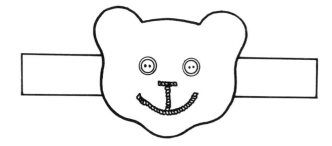
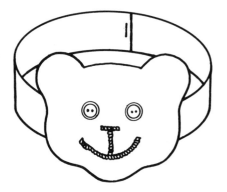

fig. 6

## Honey Pots (Loot Bags)

These are to be filled with take-home party favors for each child. Choose the type that best suits your party plans and budget.

### Pails

Buy inexpensive plastic pails with handles for each child. You may wish to print the word "honey" on them to decorate them.

### Yogurt Containers

**Materials:**
1 500 g yogurt or cottage cheese container per child
1 pipe cleaner per child
Construction paper, wrapping paper scraps
Glue
Felt pens
Single-hole punch

**Directions:**
1.  Give the children one container each, and have them decorate it by gluing on paper scraps and coloring them using the felt pens.
2.  With the help of an adult, they should punch two holes, one on each side, at the top of their containers.
3.  The pipe cleaner can then be inserted through each hole, twisting the ends to secure them, to form the handle for the container (fig. 7).

## Paper Bags

**Materials:**
1 honey pot tracer per child (fig. 16), cut out of heavy construction paper
2 pieces each of heavy colored construction paper
1 white paper lunch bag per child
Felt pens, crayons and pencils
Scissors
Glue

**Directions:**
1.  Using the honey pot tracer, have the children trace two honey pots onto their construction paper.
2.  Each child should cut out and decorate the two honey pots, using felt pens or crayons.
3.  The decorated honey pots should then be glued, one on each side of the white paper lunch bag. This is what the completed bag will look like.

fig. 7

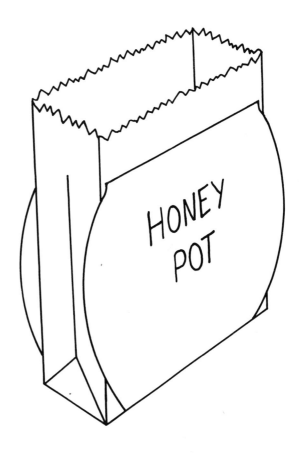

fig. 8

## Teddy Bear's Picnic

Teddy bears brought by the children may be placed on a blanket in a circle. The blanket may be set with plastic/paper cups, plates and utensils so the bears can have their own picnic while the "human" guests enjoy their lunch.

## Party Menu

The menu should be planned with the birthday child, to include the child's favorite foods.

### Bears on a Log

Wash and cut pieces of celery. Fill with peanut butter or process cheese spread. Place several raisins (bears) on the top.

### Peanut Butter and Honey Sandwiches

You may wish to cut these in fancy shapes with cookie cutters, or in circles to resemble a bear face. Open-faced circles can be decorated with raisins for facial features.

### "Beary" Juice

Serve any favorite juice.

### Teddy Bear Cake

Your favorite two-layer cake mix or homemade cake can be used. Enough batter to fill a 21-cm (8″) round pan and 23-cm (9″) square pan is required. After the cake is baked, assemble it as shown in fig. 10. When icing the cake, mix in 3 cups of coconut to give a furry texture to the bear. Decorate according to figure 10.

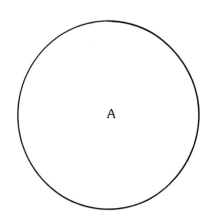

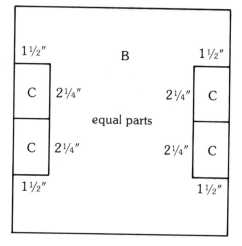

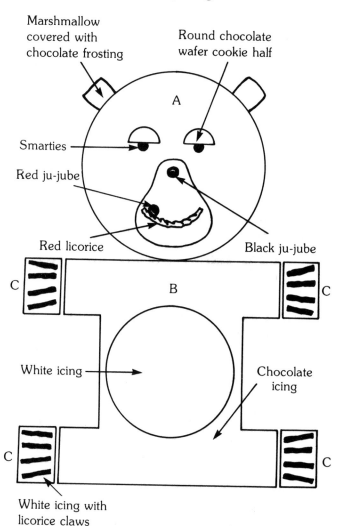

fig. 10

# Party Schedule

The schedule will vary with the age of the children, so the following is a guideline only.

| | | |
|---|---|---|
| Arrival of children | 10-15 minutes | Have a variety of children's toys or a craft (e.g. placemats) ready for the arriving guests. |
| Story | 10 minutes | To set the theme of the party, read the children a story selected from the suggested list. |
| Game 1 | 5 minutes | Teddy Bear, Teddy Bear |
| Game 2 | 10 minutes | Teddy, Teddy, Bear |
| Favor activities | 10-15 minutes | Choose activities carefully, keeping in mind that attention spans are short at this age. One or two favors can be made. Do any favors that are required for lunch. |
| Game 3 | 5-10 minutes | Treasure Hunt |
| Birthday lunch/snack | 20 minutes | |
| Favor activities | 10-15 minutes | One or two favors can be made. |
| Opening of gifts | 15-20 minutes | |
| Free play | | |
| Distribution of honey pots (loot bags) | | |
| Departure of guests | | |

# Games

Below are some games you can play at your Teddy Bear Party.

### Game 1: Teddy Bear, Teddy Bear

Teddy Bear, Teddy Bear turn around
Teddy Bear, Teddy Bear touch the ground.
Teddy Bear, Teddy Bear show your shoe
Teddy Bear, Teddy Bear I love you.
Teddy Bear, Teddy Bear go upstairs
Teddy Bear, Teddy Bear say your prayers.
Teddy Bear, Teddy Bear turn out the light
Teddy Bear, Teddy Bear say goodnight.

Do the actions suggested by the words. The children will enjoy chanting this two or three times and acting out the words in the rhyme. They may wish to play this again at a later point in the party.

### Game 2: Teddy, Teddy, Bear

Children sit in a circle. One child is chosen to be "It." "It" walks around the circle touching each child. As each child is touched, "It" says "Teddy." At some point, "It" touches a child and says "bear" instead of "Teddy". When this is done the child touched stands up and runs around the outside of the circle. At the same time, the child who is "It" runs around the circle in the opposite direction. Both children attempt to be the first one back to the empty spot in the circle. The child touched then becomes "It" and the process is repeated until each child has had a turn.

### Game 3: Treasure Hunt

This is a game all age groups will enjoy.

Choose a set of three or four party favors (candy and small toys are best) that are to be included in the honey pots. Show the children the favors and talk about each one. Explain that they are going to close their eyes (no peeking), while you hide the favors. On your signal, the children will open their eyes and each child is to find a set of favors. If they find two of the same item, they only take one. When they have found their set of three or four favors, they sit down to indicate that they have found their "treasures." These can then be put in their honey pots for them to take home.

## Suggested Books

The following books are available in local bookstores and public libraries

|  |  | Age Group |
|---|---|---|
| Asch, Frank | *Bear's Bargain* <br> *Bear's Shadow* | 3-4 |
| Barton, Pomerantz | *Where's the Bear?* | 3 |
| Berenstain, Stan and Jan | *Berenstain Bear Series* | 4-5 |
| Deans International Publishing | *Teddy Bear's Board Books* <br> *Teddy Bear's Counting Book* <br> *Teddy Bear's ABC* | 3 |
| DuBois, William | *Bear Circus* <br> *Bear Party* | 3-5 |
| Flack, Marjorie | *Ask Mr. Bear* | 3-5 |
| Freeman, Don | *Corduroy* <br> *A Pocket for Corduroy* | 4-5 |
| Gretz, Susanna | *Teddy Bears 1 to 10* | 3 |
| Hayes, Geoffrey | *Bear by Himself* | 3-5 |
| Hale, Irina | *Brown Bear in a Brown Chair* | 5 |
| Hawkins, Colin and Jacqui | *Round the Garden* | 3-4 |
| Hill, Eric | *Good Morning Baby Bear* <br> *Baby Bear's Bedtime* | 3 |
| Martin, Bill Jr. | *Brown Bear, Brown Bear, What do you see?* | 4-5 |
| Minarik, Else | *Little Bear* <br> *A Kiss for Little Bear* <br> *Little Bear's Visit* | 5 |
| Nakantani, Chiyoko | *My Teddy Bear* | 3-4 |
| Ormondroyd, Edward | *Theodore* <br> *Theodore's Rival* | 5 |
| Pinkwater, Daniel | *Bear Picture* | 4-5 |
| Rizzoli, Dru | *10 Bears in My Bed* | 4-5 |
| Romanek, Enid | *Teddy* | 3-5 |
| Waber, Bernard | *Ira Sleeps Over* | 4-5 |

# *Thank-You Notes*

It's always a treat to receive a thank-you note. Again, your child can be included in this part of the birthday party preparation. It can be fun, and a valuable learning experience for the child.

You may decide to include the thank-you note in the guest's honey pot or mail it out after the party. By following the steps for the Teddy Bear invitations, the birthday child may make his or her own thank-you notes. To simplify the process, your child may wish to draw a face on the front of the teddy bear using felt pens or crayons, rather than decorating with wool, buttons, etc. Do what suits both you and your child. Parents may write out the child's words for the child to copy into the thank-you note, or you can simply write the words and the child can sign the card. Use your own judgment about your youngster's ability.

Dear _____

Thank you for coming to my birthday party.

(add details about gifts received here, or any other appropriate message)

From

Child's name

"We hope you had a beary nice time"

fig. 11

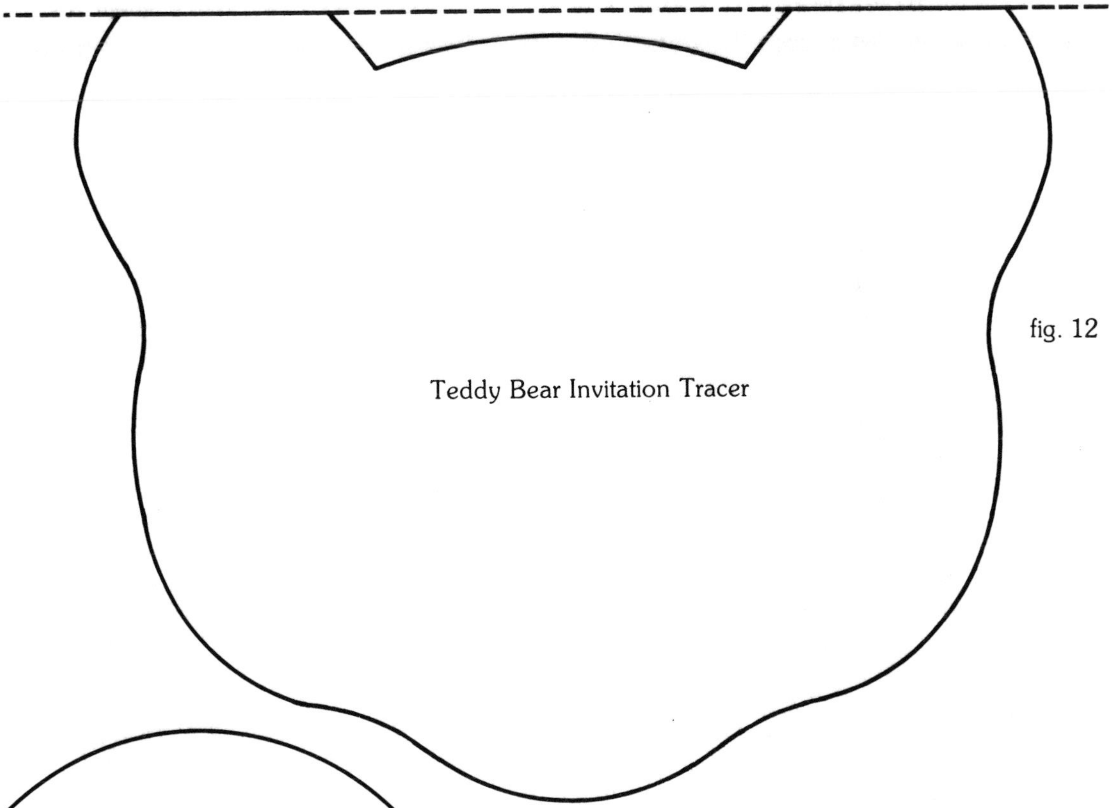

Teddy Bear Invitation Tracer

fig. 12

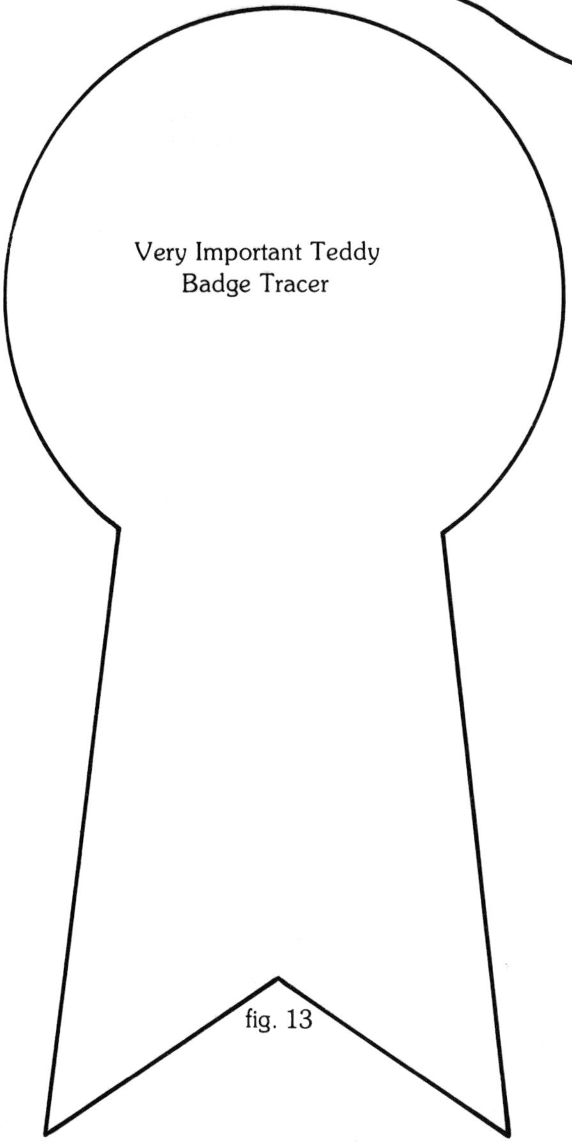

Very Important Teddy
Badge Tracer

Teddy Bear Party Hat Tracer

fig. 13

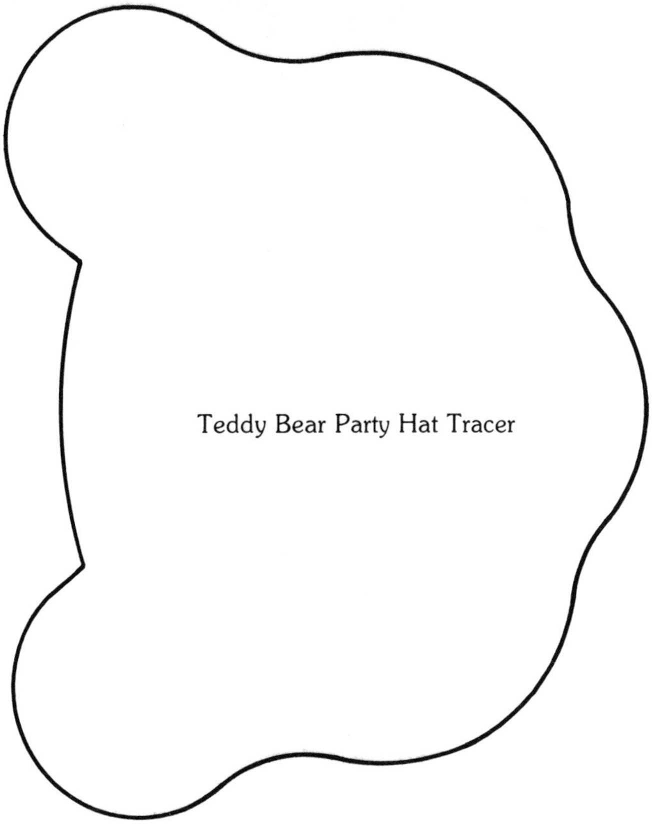

fig. 14

Teddy Bear Placemat Tracer

fig. 15

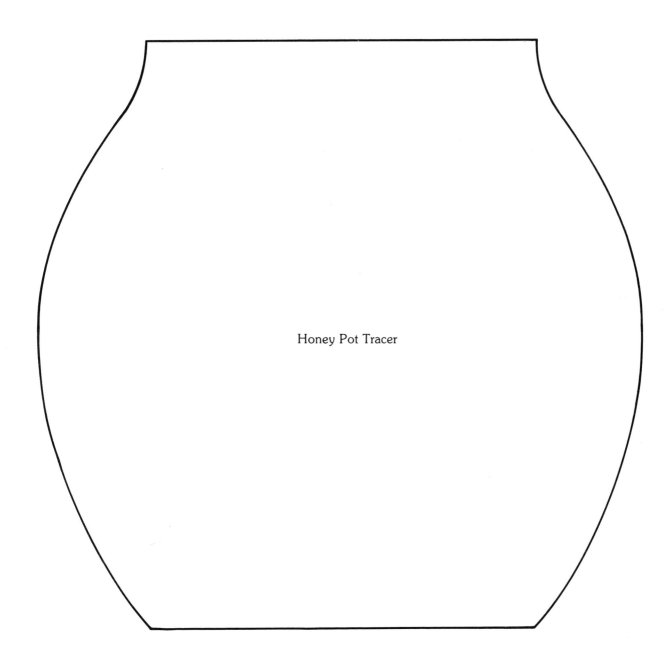

Honey Pot Tracer

fig. 16

# Space Adventure

*"Planet for any age"*

# Space Adventure

Explorations to the moon and voyages around the earth are intriguing to any youngster.

This party theme allows the children to join in the excitement of a space adventure to the moon as an astronaut. They will have their own space packs to take home, full of gear for blasting off.

They will remember this party for a long time afterwards as they role-play their own "space adventures" at home.

## Invitations

By following the directions below, you and your child can create your own Space invitation that will entice all of your guests to join you in your Space Adventure.

### Materials:
Colored construction paper
Felt pens
Scissors
Glue
Any of: silver/gold stars, colored stickers in the shape of stars, the moon, the planets or the sun (circles), tin foil

### Directions:
**1.** Cut a 37 cm × 14 cm rectangle from colored construction paper and fold it in half. Invitation now measures $18^1/_2$ cm × 14 cm.

**2.** Place the rocket tracer (fig. 14) on the foldline and trace pattern. Cut out traced rocket, cutting through both pieces of construction paper at the same time. Do not cut along the top of the rocket which is on the foldline (fig. 2).

**3.** Decorate the front of the invitation using felt pens, colored stickers, silver/gold stars, or tin foil (fig. 1).

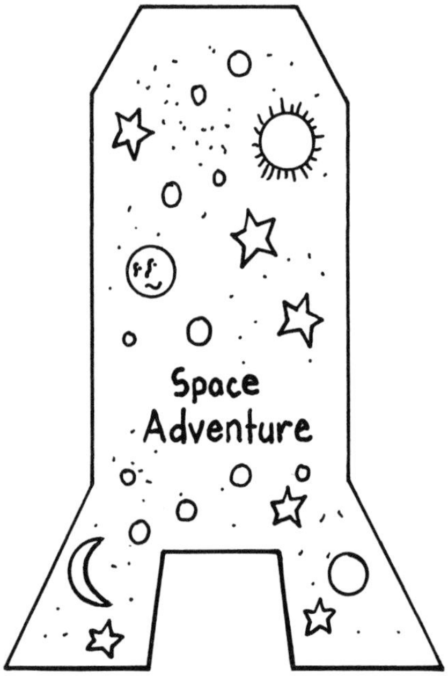

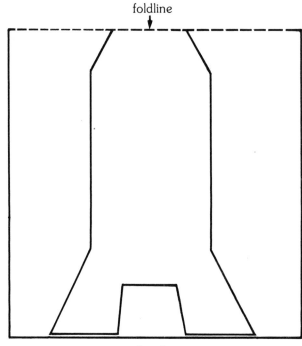

fig. 1

fig. 2

**4.** With bold pen, print "Space Adventure" clearly on the front of the invitation (fig. 1) and the all-important party details inside (fig. 3).

**5.** Distribute the invitations a week to 10 days before the party—slightly earlier if mailing.

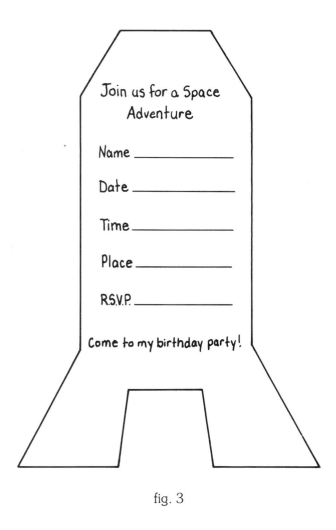

Join us for a Space
Adventure

Name _____

Date _____

Time _____

Place _____

R.S.V.P. _____

Come to my birthday party!

fig. 3

## Decorations

To create a feeling of being in space, cardboard stars made from the star tracer (fig. 13) and covered with tin foil can be hung from the ceiling or attached to the wall in the party area. Various sizes of styrofoam balls painted to resemble planets can be suspended from the ceiling. A black tablecloth, made of material or garbage bags, and decorated with the tin foil stars, will add to the outer-space atmosphere. A globe and/or toy rockets and space creatures can be used as a table centerpiece.

## Party Favors

Guests will enjoy making their own Space Packs, which will serve as loot bags to carry the party favors home in. Talk to the children about what an astronaut needs in space and this will lead into many of the favor activities. You and your child can decide on the favors you wish to include in the Space Packs.

*Party Favors You Can Buy:*

Balloons
Bubbles
Silver/gold stars
Parachutes with plastic men attached
Toy airplanes or rockets
Small bars of soap
Dried fruit
Packages of freeze-dried food
Small flashlights

*Party Favors You Can Make:*

Be sure to have children print their names on whatever they make. Each favor can then be put in the Space Packs.

### Space Packs *(Loot Bags)*

Do steps 1, 2 and 3 ahead of time to prepare for your party.

**Materials:**
One 2-litre milk carton per child
Colored construction paper
Stapler
Crayons, felt pens
Single-hole punch
String, wool, or ribbon

**Directions:**
**1.** Cut the top off each milk carton.
**2.** Using staples, cover each carton on all sides with colored construction paper.
**3.** Hole-punch two holes at the top on one side and attach a string, wool, or ribbon long enough to go over a child's head. Knot at the end (fig. 4).

**4.** At the party, each child can complete the Space Pack by decorating the outside of the pack with felt pens or crayons.

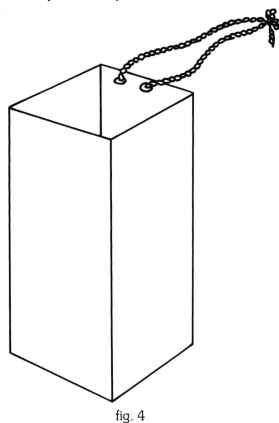

fig. 4

## Face Cloths

This face cloth, together with a small bar of soap, will be an ideal item for your astronauts to take on their Space Adventure.

**Materials:**
1 piece of white cotton cloth per child, 10 cm × 10 cm
1 piece of white paper per child, 10 cm × 10 cm
Fabric crayons (these are available at school supply stores)
Iron

**Directions:**
**1.** On the 10 cm × 10 cm white paper, each child can draw a space picture with fabric crayons. The bolder the child colors, the more it will stand out on the cloth.
**2.** The paper is then put face down on the piece of white cotton.

**3.** Using a hot iron, iron over the white paper. The heat will melt the crayon and the picture will be transferred onto the material.

## Binoculars

For almost any age!

**Materials:**
2 toilet paper rolls per child
Wool, string, or ribbon
Felt pens
Scissors
White glue

**Directions:**
**1.** Using felt pens, each child can decorate two toilet paper rolls.
**2.** The child then glues two toilet paper rolls together (fig. 5).
**3.** A string, wool or ribbon is measured and cut long enough for it to go through the rolls and over the child's head. Knot string at the end (fig. 5).

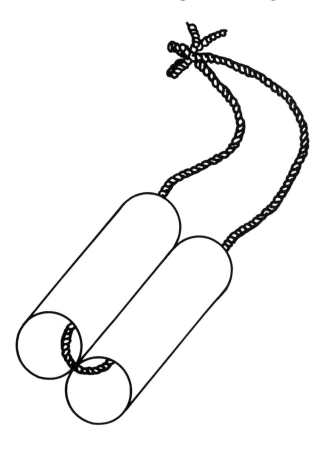

fig. 5

## *Oxygen Tanks*

These can be made by you and your child before the party, or left for older children to make at the party.

**Materials:**
One styrofoam egg carton per child
Tin foil

**Directions:**
1.   Cut the lid off the egg carton.
2.   Cover the rest of the egg carton (where the eggs sat) with tin foil. Be sure to press foil in and around each egg cup.
3.   Staple the "oxygen tank" to the front of the Space Pack (fig. 6).

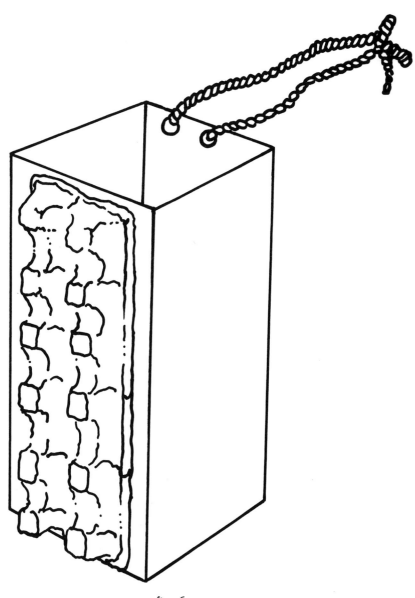

fig. 6

## *Party Schedule*

Be especially flexible with the time allowed for each activity, as it may vary with the needs and interests of the group of children.

| | | |
|---|---|---|
| Arrival | 10-15 minutes | Children can decorate their Space Packs. Have a variety of space books out for the children to browse through. |
| Story | 10 minutes | To set the theme of this Space Adventure, select a story from the suggested list and read it to the children. |
| Game 1 | 5-10 minutes | "We're Flying To The Moon." Have the verses of this game on index cards, to help you lead the children through the song. |
| Favor activities | 10-15 minutes | Oxygen Tanks (make these now if you have not prepared them before the party) Face Cloths |
| Favor activity | 10-15 minutes | Binoculars |
| Birthday lunch/snack | 20 minutes | |
| Games 2 and 3 | 15-20 minutes | Moon Walk Rings Around Saturn Do one or both as time allows. |
| Opening of gifts | 15-20 minutes | |
| Free play | | |
| Distribution of Space Packs | | |
| Departure of guests | | |

## *Games*

### *Game 1: We're Flying To The Moon*
(tune: "The Farmer in the Dell")

All children join hands in a circle in a squatting position and begin the countdown.

10, 9, 8, 7, 6, 5, 4, 3, 2, 1, 0, Ignition, **BLAST OFF!**

The countdown is chanted loudly and the children slowly rise as it proceeds. At the words "BLAST OFF," arms should be raised toward the sky. As the song begins, the children move in a clockwise direction until the end of the first verse.

*Verse 1:* We're flying to the moon, we're flying to the moon, we've left the earth in our rocket ship, and we're flying to the moon.

*Verse 2:* We're taking a walk in space, we're taking a walk in space, we've left the earth in our rocket ship, and we're taking a walk in space.

*(Drop hands and all begin the exaggerated motion of a "space walk.")*

*Verse 3:* We're landing on the moon, we're landing on the moon, we've left the earth in our rocket ship, and we're landing on the moon.

*Verse 4:*  We're walking on the moon, we're walking on the moon, we've left the earth in our rocket ship, and we're walking on the moon.

*Verse 5:*  (Countdown is repeated exactly as at the beginning of the game, as group prepares to "BLAST OFF" from the surface of the moon.)

*Verse 6:*  We're flying back to earth, we're flying back to earth, we've left the moon in our rocket ship, and we're flying back to earth.

*(Group moves in a counterclockwise direction with hands joined.)*

*Verse 7:*  We're splashing down in the sea, we're splashing down in the sea, we've left the moon and outer space, and we're splashing down in the sea.

*(With hands at sides, the children slowly fall into the sea.)*

## Game 2: Moon Walk

This game is similar to musical chairs.

**Materials:**
Star tracer (fig. 5)
Popcorn balls (see recipe)*
Tape or record
Tape recorder or record player
Construction paper
Felt pens
Scissors
Masking tape
Basket or bag
* Before the party, make one popcorn ball per child. These are the "moons" for the game.

### Caramel Syrup Recipe
Melt
    30 mL (2 tablespoons) butter
Add
    375 mL (1½ cups) brown sugar
    90 mL (6 tablespoons) water
Stir these until dissolved. Bring to boil. Cover and cook for about 3 minutes. Uncover and cook, without stirring, until a small amount dropped into cold water forms a ball.

    Makes enough for 6 cups of popcorn.

**1.**  Pop enough popcorn for each child to have 1½ cups (125 mL or ½ cup of corn yields about 4 cups when popped).

**2.**  Make the Caramel Syrup.

**3.**  When syrup is cool enough to handle, pour over popcorn in a large bowl and mix with a wooden spoon.

**4.**  Rub a small amount of butter over your hands.

**5.**  Using about 375 mL (1½ cups) of popcorn per ball, shape mixture into a ball.

**6.**  Wrap each ball in plastic wrap to keep it fresh.

**Directions:**
Using the star tracer, trace and cut two stars per child, giving you two sets. Number each set of stars, beginning at one. Tape one set of stars to the floor, forming a circle. Keep the duplicate set of stars in a basket or bag.

    To begin the game, each child stands on a numbered star on the floor. As the music plays, the children walk around the circle. When the music stops, each child stands on a star. You or a child pick a numbered star from the set of stars in the basket. The child who is standing on that number gets a "moon" (popcorn ball). This star is then taken off the floor and the pair discarded. The child can now watch the others complete the game. Moon Walk continues until everyone receives their "moon."

## Game 3: Rings Around Saturn

**Materials:**
4 golf balls or similar-sized balls
16 rubber jar rings, 4 per child
Masking tape

**Directions:**
Have four children at a time stand behind a line (made from masking tape) on the floor. Place golf balls on a carpeted area, approximately 3 feet away from the line. Each child tosses rings at the ball to see how many rings will loop Saturn.

## Suggested Books

The following books are available in bookstores and libraries.

| | | Age Group |
|---|---|---|
| Asch, Frank | *Star Baby* | 3-4 |
| | *Moon Baby* | 3-4 |
| Bentley, Roy | *Moonquake* | 7-8 |
| Freeman, Don | *Space Witch* | 4-8 |
| Freeman, Mae and Ira | *You Will Go to the Moon* | 5-7 |
| Greene, Carla | *I Want to be a Space Pilot* | 5-8 |
| Holl, Adelaide | *Moon Mouse* | 3-6 |
| Keats, Ezra Jack | *Regards to the Man in the Moon* | 4-6 |
| Udry, Janice | *The Moon Jumpers* | 4-6 |
| Ungerer, Tomi | *Moon Man* | 4-7 |
| Wise Brown, Margaret | *Goodnight Moon* | 3-6 |
| Zaffo, George J. | *The Giant Book of Things in Space* | 6-8 |

## Party Menu

Pick and choose from these galaxy goodies to make a lunch/snack that is out of this world.

### Cheese Rocket Sandwiches

Prepare $1\frac{1}{4}$ grilled cheese sandwiches for each child.

Assemble each sandwich to look like a rocket ship, using cheese triangles for the fins (fig. 7).

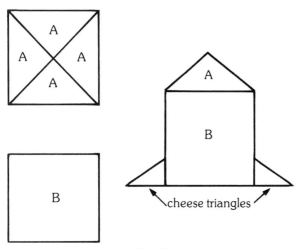

fig. 7

### Planet Creations

Children will enjoy creating their own pizzas, using a variety of toppings, on small pizza crusts, English muffins, hamburger bun halves, or a whole pita bread.

### Satellites

Mix one small package of cream cheese with 5 mL (1 tsp.) salad dressing and shape into balls. Roll in sesame seeds. Chill 30 minutes. Poke pretzel sticks into the balls.

### Milky Way Drink

Prepare chocolate milk and float miniature marshmallows in it.

### Astronaut Drink

Your child's favorite drink can be served in small plastic bags with a straw inserted at the top and secured with an elastic or twist tie.

## Rocket Ship Cake

Using your favorite cake mix or recipe, bake two
23 cm × 30 cm (9″ × 12″) cakes. Cut according
to (fig. 8). Ice and decorate (fig. 10).

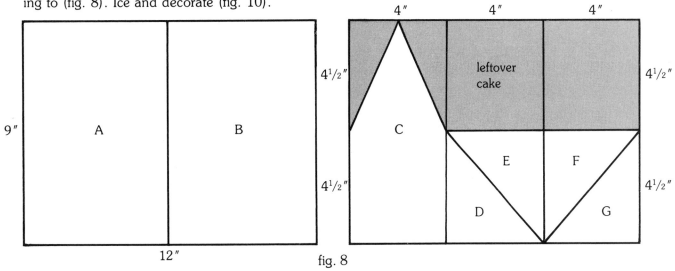

fig. 8

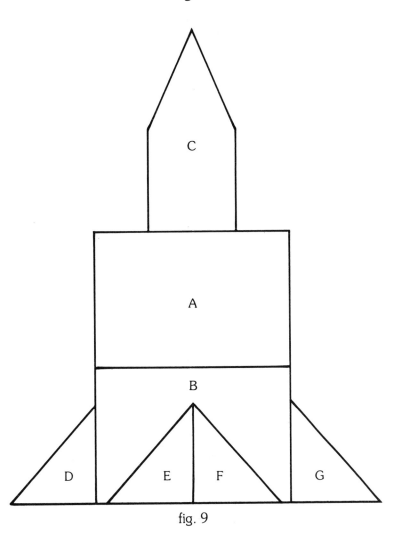

fig. 9

fig. 10

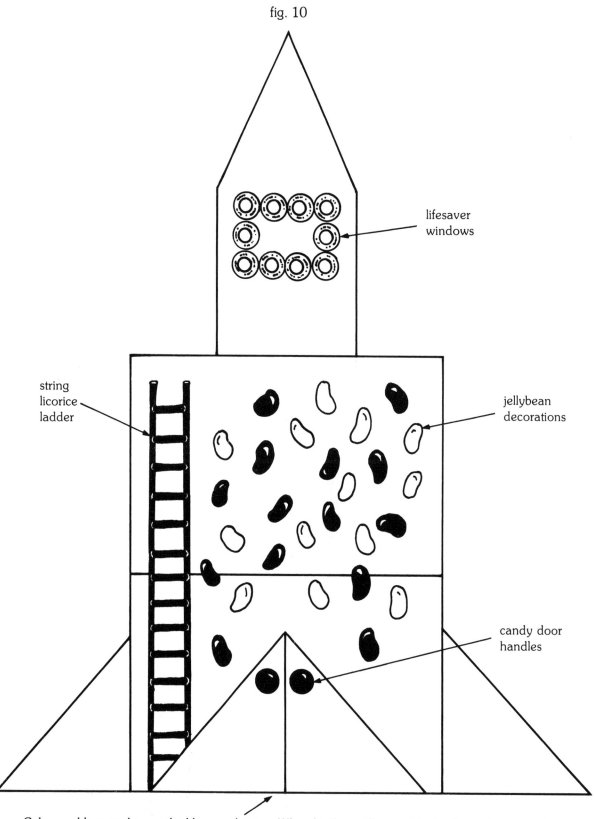

lifesaver
windows

string
licorice
ladder

jellybean
decorations

candy door
handles

Cake sparklers can be attached here with icing. When lit, they will resemble the flames from a rocket blasting off.

## *Thank-You Notes*

Sending a thank-you note is an ideal way for your child to show appreciation to the guests.

You may want to include the thank-you note in the guest's Space Pack or mail it after the party. By using the rocket ship (fig. 14) or the star tracer (fig. 12), you can create a Space Thank-You Note that contains a simple message and reminds the party guests of the day's theme.

Your child can trace and cut the thank-you notes from colored construction paper. These can be decorated if your child wishes. You or your child can print the thank-you message on the star and your child can then sign it (fig. 11).

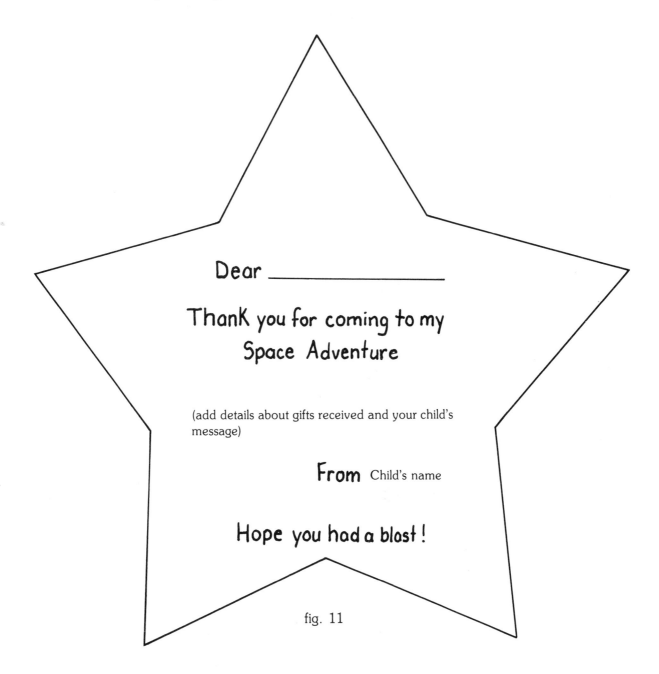

Dear _____

Thank you for coming to my
Space Adventure

(add details about gifts received and your child's message)

From Child's name

Hope you had a blast!

fig. 11

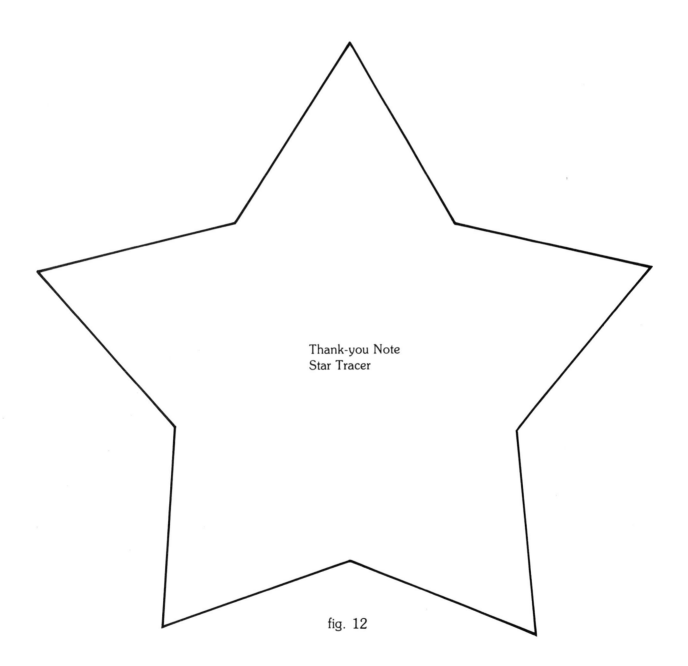

Thank-you Note
Star Tracer

fig. 12

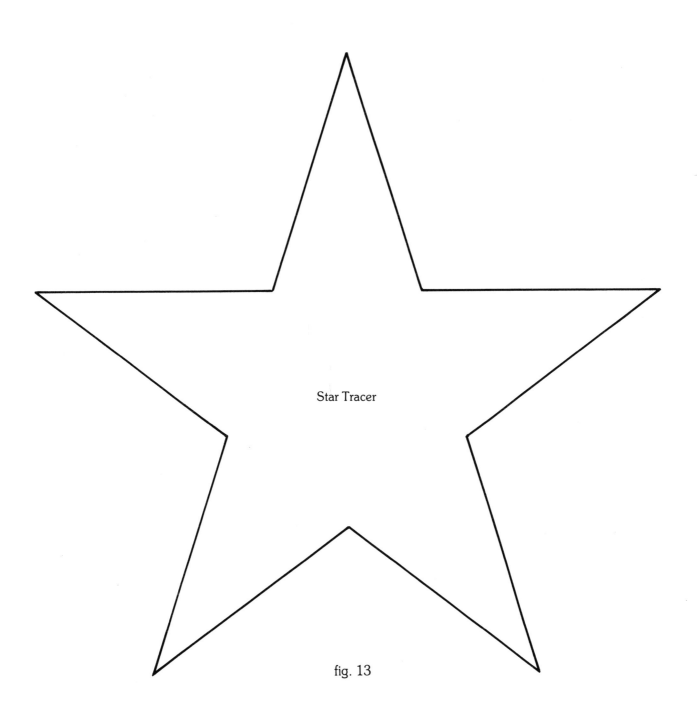

Star Tracer

fig. 13

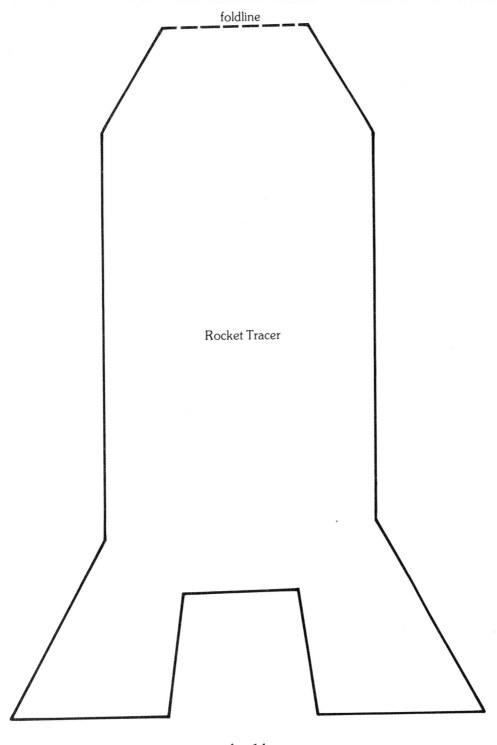

fig. 14

# A Dinosaur Trek

Just as children are captivated by the future, they also wonder about the past. Children's enthusiasm and curiosity will be sparked when dinosaurs are discussed. So much has been discovered about dinosaurs, yet so much remains unsolved.

During this party, the children can learn dinosaur names, go on a dinosaur trek and enjoy many dinosaur-related crafts and dinosaur delicacies.

## Invitations

The following is a step-by-step procedure for making your own Dinosaur Footprint invitations. Your child will enjoy making the invitations as part of the birthday celebration.

**Materials:**
Colored construction paper
Crayons, felt pens
Scissors

**Directions:**
**1.** Fold construction paper in half to fit dinosaur footprint tracer (fig. 11). Place dinosaur footprint tracer on foldline and trace the pattern. Cut out traced footprint cutting through both pieces of construction paper at the same time. Do not cut across the rounded edge of the footprint.
**2.** Decorate the invitation by outlining the footprint and drawing in claws. This may be done with crayons or felt pens.
**3.** With a bold pen, clearly print all important party details inside the invitation (fig. 3).
**4.** Hand out the invitations a week to 10 days before the party—slightly earlier if mailing.

## Decorations

To set the scene, use the dinosaur footprint tracer (fig. 11) and trace several footprints. Put these on the walls leading to and around the party area. Brown and green streamers can make a party room look swamp-like. Place several rows of brown streamers side by side going up the wall. Tape green streamers from the top of the brown streamers to the centre of the ceiling to create a palm tree. Make several of these. For a table

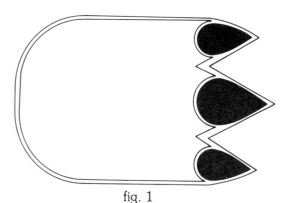

fig. 1

fig. 2

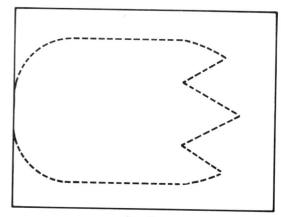

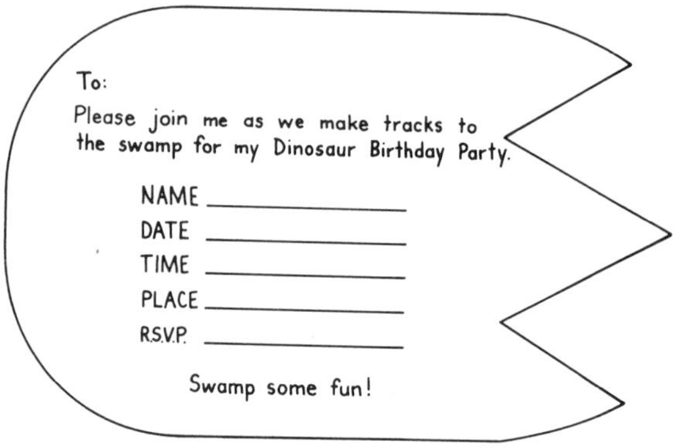

To:
Please join me as we make tracks to the swamp for my Dinosaur Birthday Party.

NAME _____
DATE _____
TIME _____
PLACE _____
R.S.V.P. _____

Swamp some fun!

fig. 3

centrepiece use a large plastic dinosaur, or a dinosaur skeleton model, both of which are available at most childrens' or teachers' supply stores. White paper placemats may be decorated with a few purchased dinosaur stickers, or children may wish to decorate the placemats themselves.

# Party Favors

This theme is designed for older children. However, you may adjust many of the activities to make them suitable for younger children. Use your own judgment to decide the favors you will buy and the ones you will have the children make. Remember, even older children may not want to make all of the party favors listed.

*Party Favors You Can Buy:*

Small plastic dinosaur figures
Dinosaur cookie cutters
Dinosaur ink stamp and stamp pad
Dinosaur stickers
Dinosaur books (see the recommended list at the end of this section)
Candy "chicken bones" (we'll rename them dinosaur bones)
Dinosaur erasers

*Party Favors You Can Make:*

Be sure to have all the children print their names on whatever they make.

## Dinosaur Eggs

These may be taken home in the Dinosaur Head Loot Bags or eaten as part of the birthday luncheon.

**Materials:**
1 hard-boiled egg per child
Crayons
2 or 3 bowls of food coloring mixture
Vinegar
1 spoon per child

**Directions:**
**1.** Before the party, hard-boil one egg per child and store them in the fridge.
**2.** Give each child an egg and have them decorate it using crayons.

**3.** Have the children gently set their decorated egg, using a spoon, in the food coloring mixture of their choice: 5 mL (1 tsp.) vinegar, 125 mL (½ cup) hot water, 20 drops of food coloring.
**4.** Remove egg from food coloring mixture when desired color is obtained, and set in a styrofoam egg carton to dry.
**5.** Put children's initials on the outside of the egg cups that hold their eggs.

## Tyrannosaurus Rex Tooth Necklace

If you decide to make this party favor, do so early in the party so that they can be baked and strung before the children leave.

**Materials:**
1 batch of Baker's Playdough (see recipe below)
Wax paper
Pencil
1 piece of thick wool or ribbon per child, about 80 cm long

**Baker's Playdough Recipe**
500 mL (2 cups) flour
250 mL (1 cup) salt
250 mL (1 cup) water
Knead until smooth. Put in bowl and cover with plastic wrap until needed.

fig. 4

**Directions:**
**1.** Give each child a piece of wax paper to work on and a ball of playdough about the size of a small orange.
**2.** Have each child make dough into 3 to 5 large dinosaur teeth. The thicker the tooth, the less chance of breakage.
**3.** With a pencil, the children can poke a hole in the top of each tooth.
**4.** Place the completed tooth on a cookie sheet and bake in the oven at 150°C (300°F) for 40 minutes.

**5.** After allowing the teeth to cool, have each child string them on the pieces of thick wool or ribbon. To keep the teeth from sliding together, the children should tie a knot between each tooth (fig. 4).

**6.** Knot each child's piece of wool or ribbon to form a necklace that slips comfortably over his or her head. Cut off excess wool or ribbon.

## Dinosaur Stick Puppets

You may wish to make a set of five Dinosaur Stick Puppets to use for Game 2 before the party and/or have each child make one for the Dinosaur Head Loot Bag.

**Materials:**
1 piece of colored construction paper per child, cut in a rectangle 20 cm × 8 cm
Assorted dinosaur tracers (see fig. 12)
Scissors
White glue
Felt pens, crayons, pencils
1 popsicle stick per child

**Directions:**
**1.** Give each child a piece of construction paper and a pencil. Have them choose and trace one of the dinosaur tracers. Cut out.
**2.** Their dinosaurs can then be decorated, using felt pens or crayons.
**3.** Have the children glue their dinosaur figures on popsicle sticks.

## Dinosaur Masks

A word of caution: make sure the eyeholes in these masks are extra large, so the children can see when wearing their masks.

**Materials:**
8½ × 11 piece of colored construction paper per child
Single-hole punch
Scissors
Felt pens, crayons, pencils
1 piece of thin sewing elastic per child
1 dinosaur head tracer per child (figs. 13, 14, 15)

**Directions:**
**1.** Give each child a dinosaur head tracer, to be traced onto construction paper.

**2.** Children then cut out the dinosaur heads and decorate them, using felt pens and crayons. Remember, cut out large eyeholes.
**3.** Punch one hole on each side of the dinosaur mask. Attach elastic and tie tightly enough to hold mask in place (fig. 5).

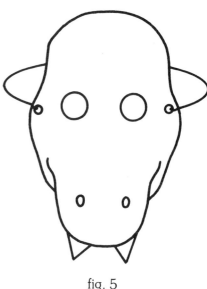

fig. 5

## Dinosaur Head Loot Bags

Children can take their party favors home in these extra-special loot bags.

**Materials:**
2 large (28 cm × 21½ cm) pieces of construction paper per child
Hole punch
Scissors
Felt pens, crayons, pencils
1 strand of wool per child 75-80 cm long
1 dinosaur-head tracer per child (fig. 16)
Stapler, staples

**Directions:**
**1.** Give each child a dinosaur head tracer and have them trace the head on both pieces of construction paper.
**2.** Have children cut out both heads and place one on top of the other. Using the hole punch, put holes along the bottom half of the dinosaur heads, placing the holes about 3 cm apart. *
**3.** Tie a knot in one end of the thick wool. The other end of the wool may be wrapped with a small piece of masking tape to make it easier for

the children to pull through the holes. By pulling the wool in and out of the holes, sew the two heads together. Bring extra wool across the top of the head and tie to knotted end of wool to form the handle.*

**4.** Have the children decorate the dinosaur heads using crayons or felt pens (fig. 6).

* Steps 2 and 3 may be too difficult for some children. An alternative would be to staple the lower half of the loot bag, punch two holes near the top and attach wool to form the handle.

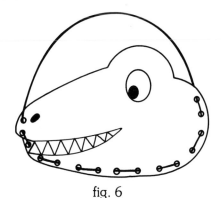

fig. 6

## Party Schedule

The following is a guideline on how to organize the party. You may wish to alter the schedule to suit the needs and interests of the children.

| | | |
|---|---|---|
| Arrival of children | 10-15 minutes | Have some toys ready for the children to play with. Begin with Tyrannosaurus Rex Tooth Necklace if you are planning to make this favor. |
| Story | 10 minutes | Reading a story will help set the mood for the party. Choose one from the suggested list. |
| Favor activities | 15 minutes | One or two favors can be made. If you plan on eating the Dinosaur Eggs for lunch these should be made at this time. Begin Dinosaur Head Loot Bags and/or Dinosaur Stick Puppets. |
| Game 1 | 15 minutes | Dino's Bingo |
| Game 2 | 5 minutes | Five Enormous Dinosaurs |
| Game 3 | 10 minutes | Dinosaur Trek |
| Birthday lunch/snack | 20 minutes | While waiting for lunch to be served, children may decorate their placemats. |
| Favor activities | 15 minutes | Complete Tyrannosaurus Rex Tooth Necklace and any other unfinished favor. Make Dinosaur Mask if time allows. |
| Opening of gifts | 15-20 minutes | |

Free play

Distribution of Dinosaur Loot Bags

Departure of party guests

# Games

Here are some suggested games you may wish to include in your party plan.

### Game 1: Dino's Bingo

This is played like regular Bingo, except the letters across the top spell D I N O S. Numbers 1 through 40 are called, and children place a marker on the number if they have it. When they have five numbers in a row, or all the numbers covered if you choose to play "blackout," they call out "Dinos." Raisins work well for markers. Winners may receive a small party favor such as a dinosaur sticker. At the end of the game, make sure each child has a sticker. See fig. 7 for a Dinos playing card. Make the number of cards you require, and print the numbers in the squares varying them from card to card. Under "D" use numbers 0-8, "I" use numbers 9-16, "N" use numbers 17-24, "O" use numbers 25-32, and "S" use numbers 33-40.

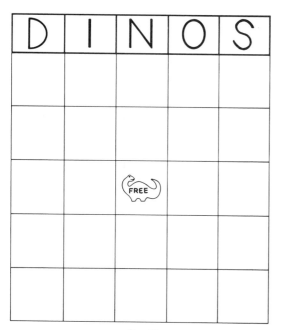

fig. 7

### Game 2: Five Enormous Dinosaurs

This is a fingerplay the children will enjoy learning. If you made a set of five Dinosaur Stick Puppets before the party, use them for this game. Have the children take turns holding up one of the puppets and taking it away. Do the verse enough times to give each child a turn. Or, if you chose not to make the set of puppets, simply have the children hold up all their fingers on one hand and put down a finger as each verse suggests.

Five Enormous Dinosaurs
Letting out a roar
One went away
And then there were four

Four Enormous Dinosaurs
Munching on a tree
One went away
And then there were three

Three Enormous Dinosaurs
Didn't know what to do
One went away
And then there were two

Two Enormous Dinosaurs
Having lots of fun
One went away
Then there was one

One Enormous Dinosaur
Not having any fun
He went away
And then there was none.

### Game 3: Dinosaur Trek

Before the party, make 10 dinosaur footprints with dinosaur footprint tracer (fig. 11). On each footprint print a simple clue such as "go look inside something near the piano" (i.e., piano bench). Print the clue in letters large enough that the children can read it together. (If the children are unable to read, read it for them.) As well, hide enough party favors, such as small dinosaur erasers, for each child.

When the game begins, tell the children they are going on a dinosaur trek together and should follow the clues on the footprints until they find a party favor. Have the children look around the room for the first clue. It is best to put this one in an obvious place so the children will notice it easily. After reading the clue, have the children look for the next footprint clue. Continue in this manner until the children have found all the hidden party favors.

# Suggested Books

The following books are available in local bookstores and public libraries.

| | | Age Group |
|---|---|---|
| Aliki | *My Visit to the Dinosaurs* | 5-8 |
| Clark, Mary Lou | *Dinosaurs* | 6-8 |
| Foreman, Michael | *Dinosaurs and All That Rubbish* | 5-8 |
| Heck, Joseph | *Dinosaur Riddles* | 5-8 |
| Hirsh, Marilyn | *The Secret Dinosaur* | 6-8 |
| Hoff, Syd | *Danny and the Dinosaur* | 4-7 |
| Holsaert, Eunice | *Dinosaurs* | 6-8 |
| Ipcar, Dahlov | *The Wonderful Egg* | 5-7 |
| Klein, Norma | *Dinosaur's Housewarming Party* | 5-8 |
| Kroll, Steven | *The Tyrannosaurus Game* | 5-8 |
| McLachlan, Edward | *Simon and the Dinosaur* | 5-8 |
| Most, Bernard | *Wherever did all the Dinosaurs Go?* | 5-8 |
| Parish, Peggy | *Dinosaur Time* | 5-6 |
| Petty, Kate | *Dinosaurs* | 5-8 |
| Reinstedt, Randall A. | *Dinosaur Dan* | 7-8 |
| Roberts, Sarah | *The Adventures of Big Bird in Dinosaur Land* | 3-5 |
| Thayer, Jane | *Quiet on Account of Dinosaur* | 6-8 |

# Party Menu

Plan the menu with your child as they may wish to include their favorite foods. Here is a fun chant you can teach as you are serving the hungry dinosaurs.

Allosaurus, Stegosaurus,
Brontosaurus too,
All went off for dinner at the
Dinosaur Zoo
Along came the waiter
called Tyrannosaurus Rex
Gobbled up the table
'Cause they wouldn't pay their checks.

Dennis Lee,
*Jelly Belly*

### Dinosaur Bones
Cut and wash carrot and celery sticks.

### Brontosaurus Burgers
Hamburgers with any toppings you wish.

### Swamp Swill
Mix equal parts of root beer and orange pop.

### Dinosaur Eggs
The children may enjoy eating their decorated hard-boiled eggs.

## Dinosaur Bone Cake

Double your recipe for your child's favorite cake. Bake one recipe in a 23 cm × 30 cm (9″ × 13″) rectangular pan and the other in two 22 cm (9″) round layer cake pans.

Cut according to fig. 8. Ice and decorate (fig. 9).

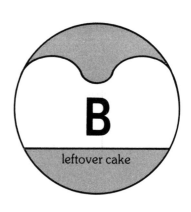

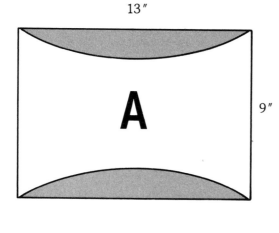

13″

9″

fig. 8

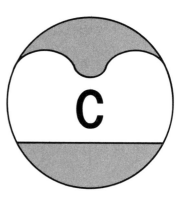

leftover cake

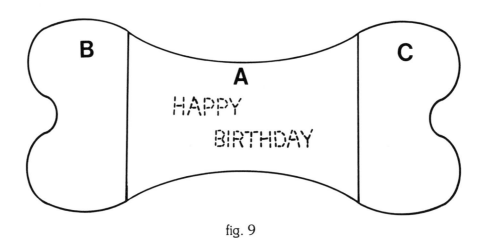

fig. 9

Ice with white icing and decorate with shredded coconut. "Happy Birthday" may be spelled out with the candy "chicken bones."

## Thank-You Notes

At this age children can be learning the importance of saying "thank-you."

You may wish to include the thank-you note in the guests' Dinosaur Loot Bags or mail it out after the party.

To make the thank-you notes, follow the same steps you used to make the Dinosaur Footprint invitations. Parents or the child may write out the words the child wishes to say inside the thank-you note and then the child may sign his or her name.

Dear _____
Thank you for coming on my Dinosaur Trek.

**From** Child's name

"I'm glad you made tracks to my birthday party."

fig. 10

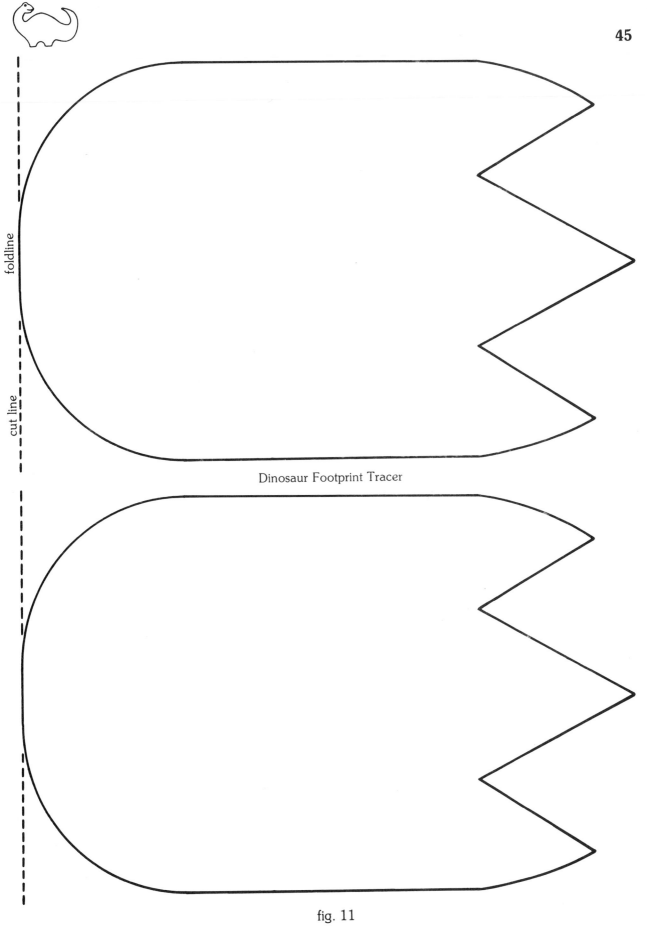

foldline

cut line

Dinosaur Footprint Tracer

fig. 11

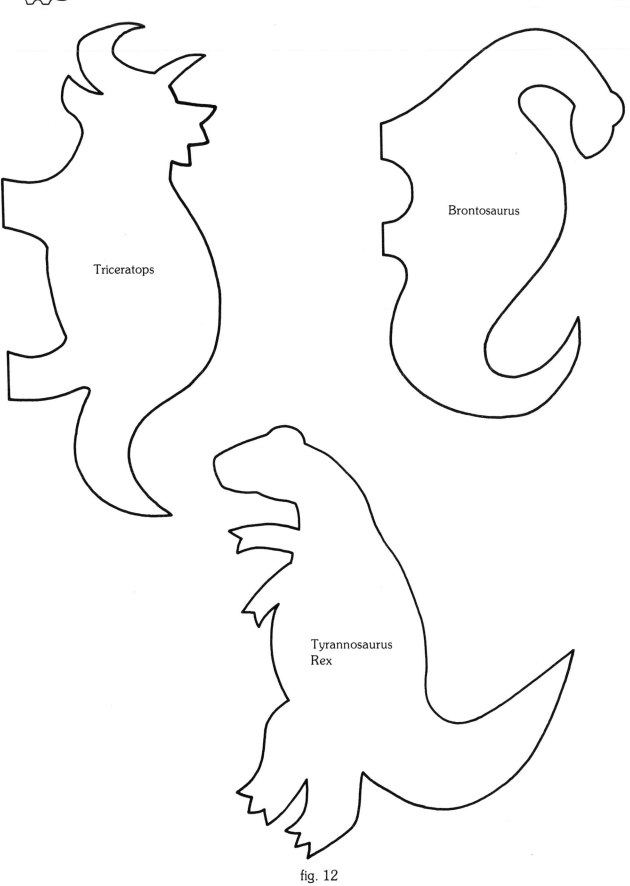

Triceratops

Brontosaurus

Tyrannosaurus
Rex

fig. 12

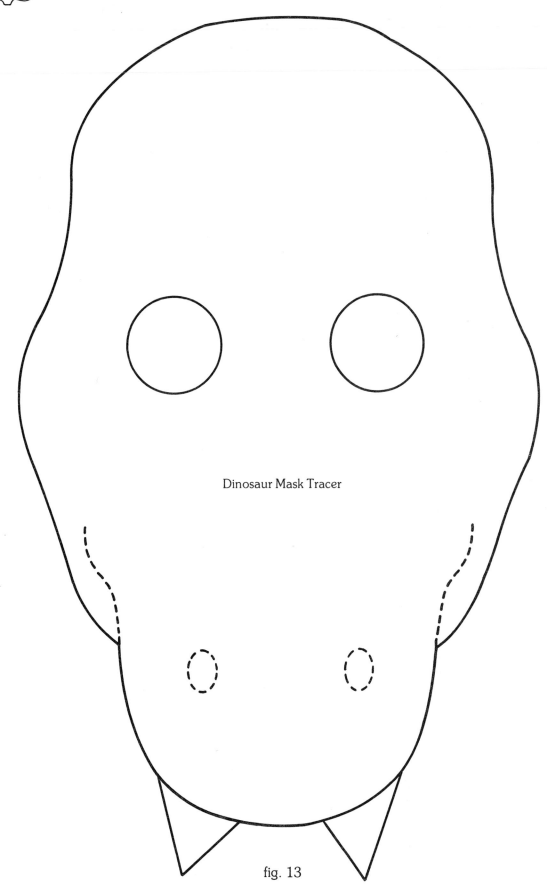

Dinosaur Mask Tracer

fig. 13

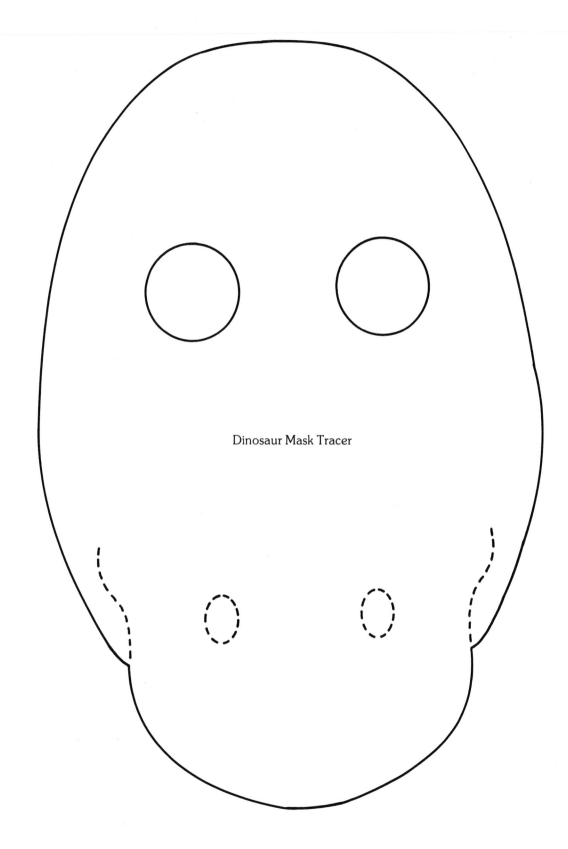

Dinosaur Mask Tracer

fig. 14

Dinosaur Mask Tracer

fig. 15

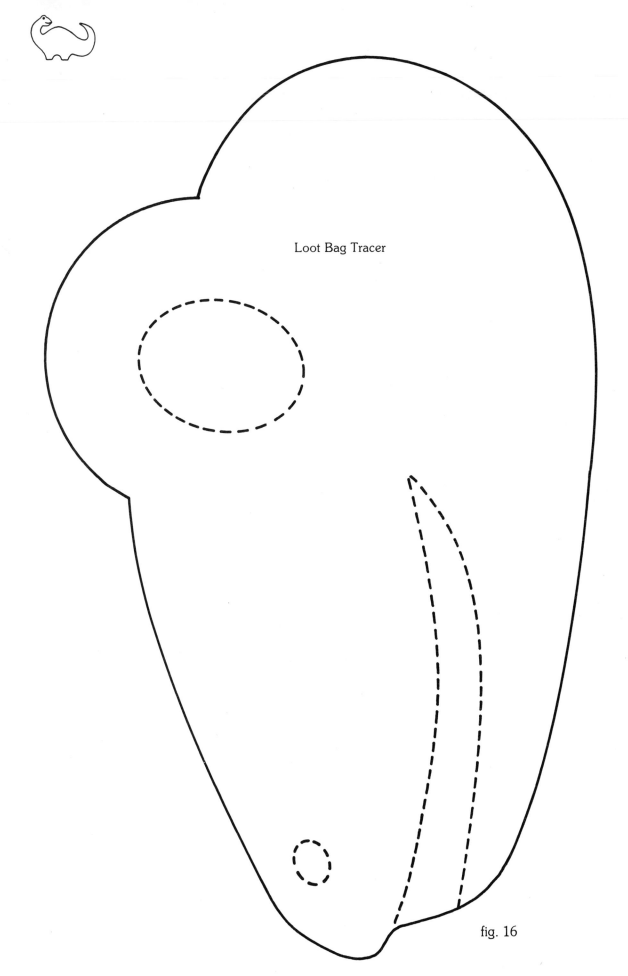

Loot Bag Tracer

fig. 16

# A Gingerbread Birthday

Children love fairy tales and one of their favorites is the Gingerbread Boy. They love repeating the Gingerbread Boy chant:

"Run, run, run, as fast as you can
You can't catch me, I'm the Gingerbread Man!"

What better way for children to enjoy a gingerbread party than to make their own gingerbread men or a gingerbread house, both of which are included in this plan, along with many craft ideas.

This theme lends itself very well to those children who celebrate their birthdays during the Christmas season. However, "visions of gingerbread dance in their heads" any time of the year!

## Invitations

Invitations are the first step in preparing for your Gingerbread Party.

**Materials:**
Colored construction paper
Crayons, felt pens
Scissors
Glue
Jelly beans or gumdrops

**Directions:**
1. Fold construction paper in half to fit gingerbread tracer (fig. 17). Place gingerbread tracer on the foldline and trace pattern. Cut out traced gingerbread house, cutting through both pages at the same time. Do not cut across the roof of the house.

2. Decorate your gingerbread house by drawing on a door, chimney, and curtains. You can also draw on imaginary icing sugar, candied bricks and other yummy decorations. You may wish to glue a gumdrop or jelly bean on, as a door knob. Cut one layer along cut line for door (fig. 2).

3. With a bold pen, print clearly all important party details inside each invitation (fig. 3).

4. Distribute your party invitations a week to 10 days before the party—slightly earlier if mailing.

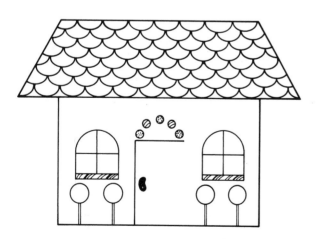

fig. 1

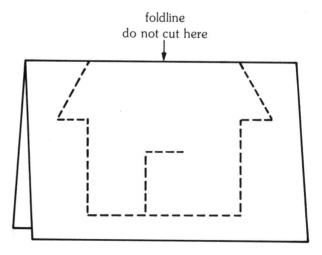

foldline
do not cut here

fig. 2

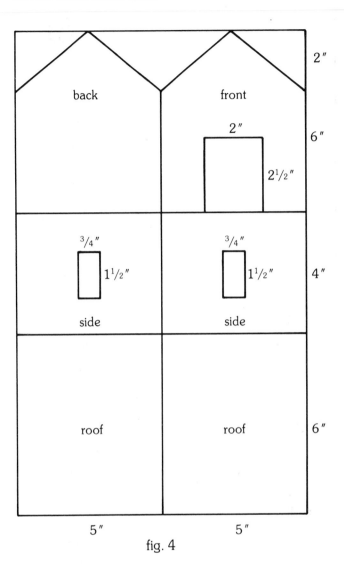

You are invited to my "Land of Gingerbread Birthday Party

NAME _____
DATE _____
TIME _____
PLACE _____
R.S.V.P. _____

Here comes the Gingerbread man!

fig. 3

## Decorations

In keeping with the gingerbread theme, you may wish to decorate the party room as a gingerbread house. Streamers may be hung from the doorway so that the children get the feeling of entering a special place. String popcorn and hang it on the walls and ceiling. Suckers and other wrapped candy can also be hung. Using the gingerbread man tracer (fig. 16), cut gingerbread men from brown construction paper and decorate with felt pens. These can be placed around the room.

A large gingerbread house makes a great table centerpiece. You and your child can decorate it ahead of time, or you may wish to have the party guests lend their helping hands! Following is a recipe and instructions for baking and assembling your own gingerbread house.

## Gingerbread House

125 mL ($\frac{1}{2}$ cup) oil
75 mL ($\frac{1}{3}$ cup) brown sugar, packed
1 egg
150 mL ($\frac{2}{3}$ cup) molasses
675 mL ($2\frac{3}{4}$ cup) sifted flour
2 mL ($\frac{1}{2}$ tsp.) salt
5 mL (1 tsp.) ginger
15 mL (3 tsp.) baking powder
15 mL (3 tsp.) cinnamon
.5 mL ($\frac{1}{8}$ tsp.) cloves
Mix well and chill several hours or overnight. Roll dough onto well-greased large cookie sheet. Mark and cut pattern onto uncooked dough (fig. 4). Bake at 150°C (300°F) about 35 minutes or until well done. Remove from oven and cut through

pattern markings again. Remove cut pieces from cookie sheet when cool.

fig. 4

## Royal Icing

3 egg whites
2 mL ($\frac{1}{2}$ tsp.) cream of tartar
500 g (1 lb.) icing sugar
Beat ingredients in mixing bowl until icing stands in peaks. Keep bowl covered with damp cloth, as icing hardens very quickly. Vanilla extract may be added to icing for flavor.

### Assembly:
To assemble the gingerbread house, you will need a piece of cardboard covered with foil to build on. The icing will be used as glue.
**1.** Take one side panel and spread icing along all four edges. Stand it on foiled base.

**2.** Take back panel and spread icing along all edges. Attach to side panel.
**3.** Repeat steps 1 and 2 for other side panel and front panel.
**4.** Put icing along edges of one roof panel as well as a strip underneath the edge of the roof. Place roof panel on top of the house walls and hold until set.
**5.** Repeat for other roof panel.
**6.** Cut each window piece in half and ice the four together. Place on roof as chimney.
**7.** Now have fun finishing off the house with lots of icing, decorations and assorted candies. Dip candy into icing as you go, so that the icing doesn't harden first.

## Party Favors

The Gingerbread Party lends itself to lots of baking and craft activities. Included here are ideas for a gingerbread man (bake), individual gingerbread houses (no-bake), gingerbread man necklaces or key chains (bake), gingerbread man hats and gingerbread man loot bags. Consider the age and abilities of the children at your party before you choose how much to take on. You may decide on a combination of homemade and store-bought party favors.

*Party Favors You Can Buy:*

Gingerbread man cookie cutter
Gingerbread man books
"The Gingerbread Boy"—story and small record
Gingerbread man stickers
Gingerbread man and house Christmas tree
    trimmings
Gingerbread man fridge magnets
Gingerbread man barrettes

*Party Favors You Can Make:*

## Gingerbread Man Loot Bags

You may have these ready ahead of time, or you may choose to do them at the party as one of your favor activities.

**Materials:**
Brown construction paper
1 brown lunch bag per child
Glue

Felt pens, crayons
**Directions:**
**1.** Using gingerbread man tracer (fig. 16), cut and trace one gingerbread man per child.
**2.** Each child can decorate a gingerbread man with felt pens or crayons.
**3.** Now glue each decorated gingerbread man to the front of a brown lunch bag (fig. 5).

fig. 5

## Gingerbread Man Cookies

Depending on the age of the children at the party, you can make the dough ahead of time, or make it with the children. This recipe makes at least 3½ dozen cookies.
250 mL (1 cup) melted shortening
250 mL (1 cup) white sugar
500 mL (2 cups) molasses
2 eggs, beaten
250 mL (1 cup) milk
1750 mL (7 cups) flour
25 mL (5 tsp.) baking soda
5 mL (1 tsp.) ginger
5 mL (1 tsp.) cloves
5 mL (1 tsp.) cinnamon
Mix dry and wet ingredients separately. Gradually combine them to make a workable dough.

The children can form gingerbread men by rolling balls for the heads and molding the body parts with their hands. The dough may also be rolled out ¼″ thick and cut with cookie cutters. Bake for about 8 minutes until firm and lightly browned, at 180°C (350°F). Decorate the cookies with icing, jelly beans, ju-jubes, licorice, sprinkle candies, or coconut.

## Individual Gingerbread Houses

This is an exciting and simple activity for the children to do, requiring very little assistance.

**Materials:**
Royal icing (pg. 00)
6 graham wafers per child
Candies to decorate: ju-jubes, Smarties, jelly beans
Cake sprinkles, coconut, peppermint sticks
A cardboard square 15 cm × 15 cm (6″ × 6″) per child, covered with foil, for the children to use as a base for building their houses.

**Directions:**
Each child takes a cardboard square and builds a house as follows.
1. Take one graham wafer and spread icing on all four edges. Stand up on foiled base.
2. Take another wafer, again spreading icing on all four edges. Stand against first panel so that the house has a back.
3. Repeat steps 1 and 2 to make another side and front to the house.
4. Spread icing ½″ thick around two remaining wafers, and place on top of the four walls to make a slanted roof (fig. 6).
5. Dip candies in icing and decorate the roof and four sides of the house.

## Gingerbread Necklace or Key Chain

This is a fun activity for just about any age. This recipe makes enough for eight children to prepare two each.

**Materials:**
500 mL (2 cups) flour
250 mL (1 cup) salt
250 mL (1 cup) water (or enough to make a workable dough)
30 mL (2 tbsp.) powdered tempera paint or food coloring, any colors
Ribbon or string
Toothpicks, pencils

**Directions:**
1. Mix flour, salt and water to make a good, workable playdough. Add tempera powder.
2. Separate into handfuls and give to each child.
3. Have children mold their pieces to make either gingerbread men or gingerbread houses.
4. Use toothpicks to etch on features of men and house.
5. Push a pencil through the sculpture to make a hole big enough to run a string through.
6. Bake at 120°C (250°F) for 40 minutes or until firm.
7. Cut string or ribbon long enough to make keychains or necklaces and thread through holes (figs. 7 and 8).

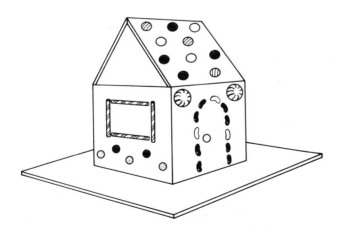

fig. 6

fig. 7

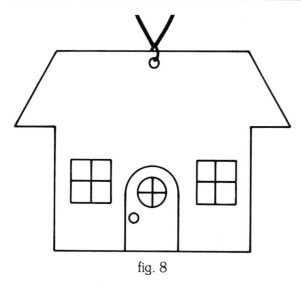

fig. 8

## Gingerbread Hats

This is an activity that may require some adult help in the cutting and folding.

**Materials:**

1 strip of light construction paper 9 cm ×
   50 cm per child
Crayons, pastels
Stapler, staples
Scissors
Gingerbread man tracer (fig. 18)

**Directions:**

**1.** Fold paper every 5 cm like an accordion, back and forth, back and forth, until all folded.
**2.** Put gingerbread tracer on top of folded paper and trace around (fig. 9).

**3.** Cut out exactly as shown. Do not cut around arms.
**4.** Open strip of paper and decorate with crayons and pastels (fig. 10).
**5.** Staple together to fit child's head. Cut off excess paper.

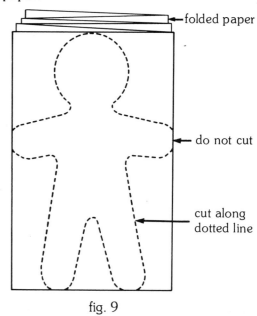

fig. 9

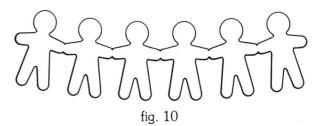

fig. 10

# Party Schedule

Choose the activities you think the children at your party would enjoy doing. Keep in mind their ages and abilities in finding "the right mix."

| | | |
|---|---|---|
| Arrival of children | 10-15 minutes | Have toys and books ready for the children to play with before the party starts. |
| Favor activities | 20-30 minutes | Choose from any of the activities. Favors that require baking should be done at this time (Gingerbread Man Cookies, Necklaces and Keychains). |
| Story—"The Gingerbread Boy" | 10 minutes | Reading this story aloud helps to set the theme of the party and leads into the first game. |

| | | |
|---|---|---|
| Game 1 | 10 minutes | Gingerbread Man Hunt (hide gingerbread men ahead of time). |
| Favor activity | 20-30 minutes | Individual Houses (these may require up to 30 minutes), Loot Bags, Hats |
| Birthday lunch/snack | 15 minutes | |
| Game 2 | 10 minutes | "Run, Run, As Fast As you Can" |
| Opening of gifts | 15-20 minutes | |
| Free play | | |
| Distribution of Gingerbread Man Loot Bags | | |
| Departure of guests | | |

## Games

### Game 1: The Gingerbread Man Hunt

This is lots of fun and will be remembered for a long time after!

You will need to have the gingerbread men (recipe, page 5) already baking in the oven when you start this game. Read the story "The Gingerbread Boy," making sure to talk about how the Gingerbread Boy jumped from the oven and got away. Meanwhile, have somebody remove the tray of baking and hide it. Have the person leave a trail of crumbs or parts of extra cookies on the floor, so that the children will see them and follow them as clues. Now, still with the children, finish the story and suggest that they check their gingerbread men. Oh! They too have jumped from the oven . . . the hunt is on!!!!

### Game 2: "Run, Run, As Fast As You Can"

Best suited for smaller parties, where there is a large amount of space available. Follow the sequence of your story.

A child is chosen to be the escaped Ginger-bread Boy. He sings:

"Run, Run as fast as you can, you can't catch me I'm the Gingerbread Man."

Next, one child is chosen to be the old woman and calls:

"I'm the old woman, I'll catch you."

This child chases the Gingerbread Man (child 1) around the room. The Gingerbread Man sings his song again:

"Run, Run, as fast as you can, you can't catch me, I'm the Gingerbread Man."

Then, another child grabs onto the waist of the old woman and calls:

"I'm the old man, I'll catch you."

And away they chase. This continues, as the Gingerbread Man returns each time to the waiting children singing his song. All the children eventually join in by being the characters in the story, until the last child picked is the fox. Eventually, the Gingerbread Boy is caught and all the children encircle him! Try it a few times, letting the children take on different roles.

## Suggested Books

The following books are available in bookstores and libraries.

| | | Age Group |
|---|---|---|
| American Folk Tale | *The Gingerbread Boy* | 3-8 |
| Daly, Niki | *Ben's Gingerbread Man* | 3-5 |
| Grimm Brothers | *Hansel and Gretel* | 3-8 |

# Party Menu

### Gingerbread House Sandwich

Make the birthday child's favorite type of sandwich. Cut corners off the sandwich to make a gingerbread house (fig. 11).

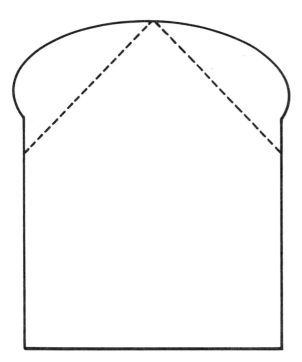

fig. 11

### Cheesy Gingerbread Men

Using a small cookie cutter, cut gingerbread men out of processed cheese slices.

### Gingerbread Faces

Apply processed cheese spread to round crackers and let the children build faces with raisins and shelled sunflower seeds.

fig. 12

### Magic Juice

Use chocolate milk or your child's favorite drink, adding a small scoop of ice cream for foam.

### Gingerbread House Cake

Using your favorite layer cake mix, bake in two 20 cm (8″) square pans. Follow the assembly directions below to cut and build your Gingerbread House Cake (figs. 13 and 14).

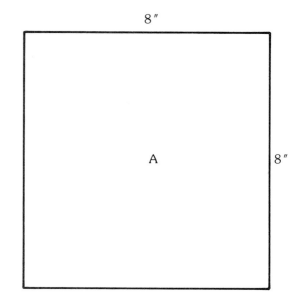

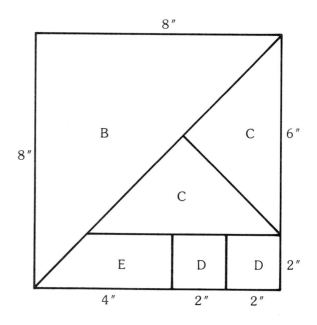

fig. 13

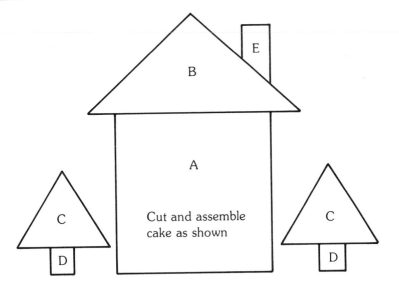

B

E

A

Cut and assemble
cake as shown

C

D

C

D

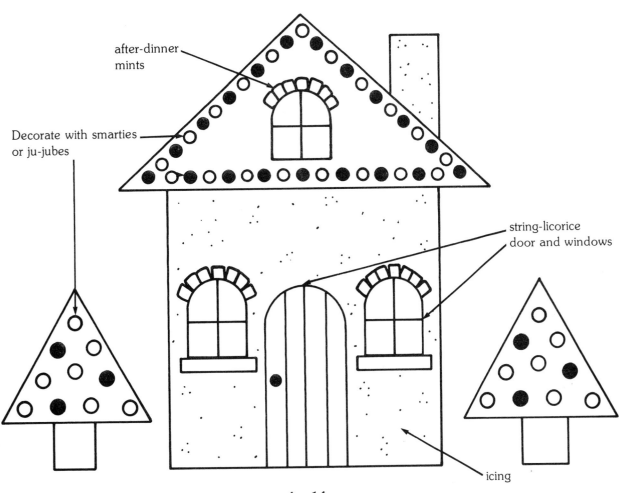

after-dinner
mints

Decorate with smarties
or ju-jubes

string-licorice
door and windows

icing

fig. 14

# Thank-You Notes

Here is an opportunity for your child to say "thank-you."

By following the steps for making the gingerbread house invitations, you can make the thank-you notes too. Your child can help decorate the thank-you notes on the outside and may also help to print the details on the inside (fig. 15). Decide how much your child is able to do and complete the birthday celebration together!

Dear _____

Thank you for coming to
my Birthday party

(add details about gifts here)

From _Child's name_

Glad you ran to the occasion!!

fig. 15

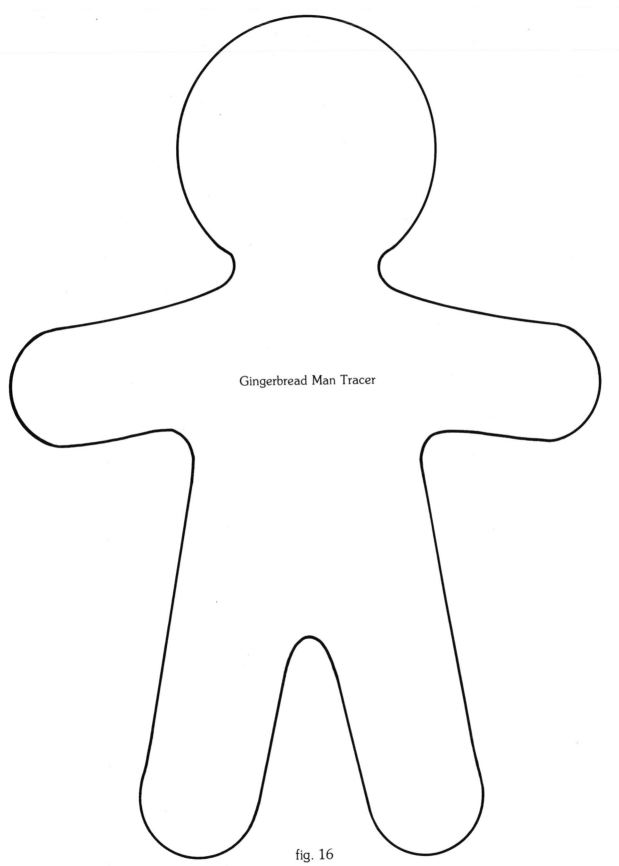

Gingerbread Man Tracer

fig. 16

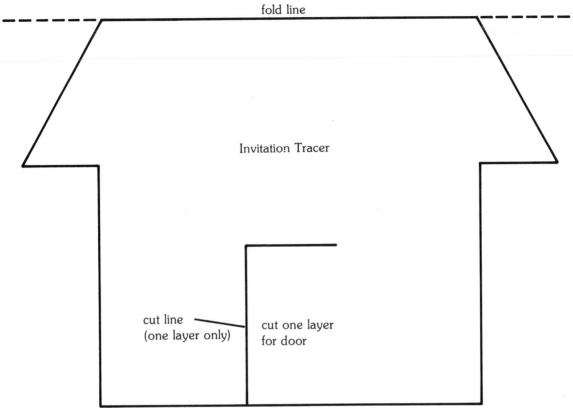

fold line

Invitation Tracer

cut line
(one layer only)

cut one layer
for door

fig. 17

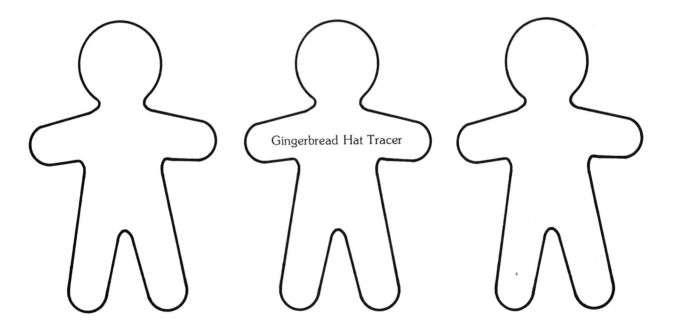

Gingerbread Hat Tracer

fig. 18

# Circus Celebration

*We nose you'll enjoy it!*

# *Circus Celebration*

"Come one, come all
Here comes the circus!"
Thoughts of the circus bring a smile to everyone's face! This popular attraction has been bringing delight to people for centuries.

You can create a circus atmosphere with the many creative activities provided in this chapter. Children will enjoy assembling their own circus train, entering a big top, making circus animal crafts and just plain clowning around!

## *Invitations*

You and your child can begin the birthday celebrations by preparing your own circus invitations. Children and adults alike will run to see the circus train come to town! The circus train is a fun and easy invitation to make.

Each invitation is a separate train car. You can then request that your guests bring their invitations to the party (add a reminder on each invitation), at which time all the cars can be joined to make a circus train. You and your child can make the engine that will begin the train. The completed train can also be used as a centerpiece for your table.

For each invitation follow the directions below.
**Materials:**
Colored construction paper
Train-car tracer (fig. 16)
Engine tracer (fig. 10)
Circus animal tracers (figs. 17-21)
Scissors
Wool, felt material
Pencil, felt pens, crayons
Glue
Sequins

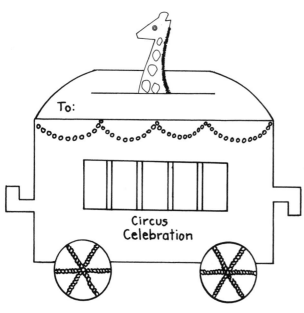

fig. 1

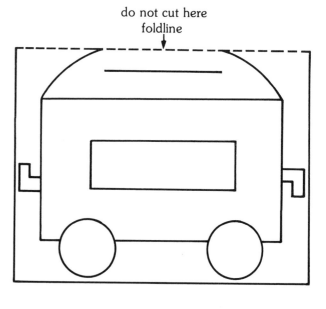

fig. 2

**Directions:**

1. Fold colored construction paper in half to fit circus train-car tracer (fig. 16). Place the train-car tracer on the foldline and trace the pattern. Cut out the traced car, cutting through both pieces of construction paper at the same time. Do not cut across the top of the car that is on the foldline (fig. 2).

2. Decorate the front of the train car using crayons, felt pens and sequins. Be sure to draw on the bars of the car. With bold pen, you or your child can clearly print the guest's name on the roof of the car and the words "Circus Celebration" on the bottom (fig. 1). Scraps of construction paper can be used to make the hook-ups.

3. Using the animal tracers (figs. 17-21), trace and cut out one animal for each invitation. A variety of animals will make your circus train more exciting when it is assembled at the party.

4. Your child will enjoy filling in animal features, using sequins, wool, felt material, crayons and felt pens. With a bold pen, print clearly the all-important party details on the animal's body (figs. 17-21).

5. With scissors, make a slit along the roof of your train car large enough to fit the animal's head through. Slip the circus animal between the front and back of the train car and through the slit on the roof, so the animal's head is visible. When the front of the invitation is opened, an animal bearing the important party details will be revealed.

6. If the children are bringing their invitations to the party, make your engine by following the directions for the train cars and using the engine tracer (fig. 22).

7. Distribute your invitations a week to 10 days before the party—slightly earlier if mailing.

fig. 3

## Decorations

All the excitement of a circus can come to life by decorating the party area to resemble a "big top." Take long, brightly colored streamers in groups of four and tape them together at one end. Attach these to the center of the ceiling. Twist each streamer and fan out to one wall. Attach along the wall. Repeat this three times, taking each set of streamers to the other three walls, so that the entire area is covered (fig. 4).

Inflate bright balloons, making sure there is one for each child at the party. These can be tied together in groups of four or five and hung in the center of the ceiling, as well as in the four ceiling corners.

Stuffed animals such as bears, lions, monkeys, elephants, dogs and horses can be placed around the room, inside hula hoops (circus rings) or behind cage bars made from streamers. Your table can be gaily decorated with your circus train, thin streamers and a few bright balloons.

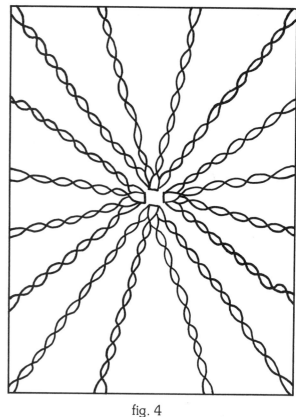

fig. 4
top view

## Party Favors

Children will pounce on these circus party favors. You and your child can decide which party favors are best for your party.

*Party Favors You Can Buy:*

Balloons
Popcorn (pop and put into small plastic
  sandwich bags)
Animal crackers
Clown birthday hats
Peanuts in the shell
Ju-jube circus animals
Clown lollipops
Circus stickers
Plastic circus animals

*Party Favors You Can Make:*

Be sure materials for each favor are ready at the beginning of your party. Children should also put their names on the party favors that they make.

## Clown Hat Loot Bags

You can purchase commercial clown hats that the children can wear at the party or the children can make their own clown hats. The hats can also be used to carry home their party favors.

**Materials:**
2 pieces of colored bristol board per child (each
  piece large enough to fit fig. 24)
Clown hat tracer (fig. 24)
Pompom (available in craft stores) or cotton
  ball, one per child
Felt pens, crayons
Scissors
Stapler, staples
Single-hole punch
1 piece of thin sewing elastic per child
Any of: glitter, sequins, different shapes of
  colored stickers

**Directions:**

**1.** Using clown hat tracer (fig. 24), children can trace a clown hat on two pieces of bristol board. Then they cut out each clown hat and staple them together along the sides and top (bottom is left open).

**2.** The pompom or cotton ball can be glued to the pointed top. The clown hat can be decorated using felt pens, crayons, colored stickers, glitter or sequins.

**3.** Punch a hole on each side of the bottom. Knot elastic in the holes as a handle (fig. 5).

## Clown Masks

Easy to make!

**Materials:**
1 white styrofoam or paper plate per child
Felt pens, crayons
Colored paper scraps
1 ball of wool
Thin sewing elastic
Single-hole punch
Glue
Scissors
Any of: glitter, sequins, colored stickers

**Directions:**

**1.** Place a styrofoam or paper plate in front of each child's face and mark where the eyes will be. Cut out eye holes with scissors.

**2.** The children can then decorate their masks as funny clown faces, using felt pens, crayons, colored paper scraps, glitter, sequins, colored stickers and wool for hair (fig. 6).

**3.** Hole-punch the two sides of the mask and tie on thin sewing elastic, so that the mask will fit comfortably on the child's face.

## Face Painting

Children will enjoy having their own faces made up to look like a clown. You can use commercial face make-up or make your own, using the following recipe.

*Be sure to ask the children's parents about allergies to either type of make-up.

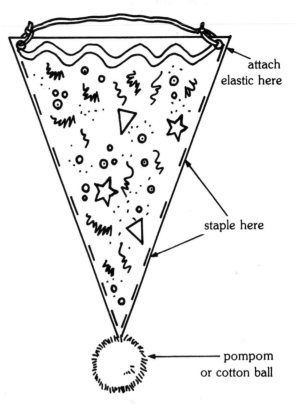

fig. 5

fig. 6

**Circus Make-Up:**
2 parts vegetable shortening
1 part cornstarch

Color with powdered tempera paint.
Use fingertips to apply.
This will come off easily!

## Paper Bag Lion Heads

With this favor, everyone can be a lion in the circus!

**Materials:**
1 large paper bag per child
Several strips of colored construction paper,
   2.5 cm × 30 cm
Scissors
Colored paper, colored stickers
Felt pens, crayons, pencils
Glue

**Directions:**
1. Place a paper bag over each child's head. Cut off or fold up the bottom of the bag to fit the child's head. Mark where the eyes will be.
2. After you cut out the eyeholes, children can add lion features, using colored paper, colored stickers, felt pens and crayons.
3. To make the lion's mane, the children can roll a strip of colored construction paper, 2.5 cm × 30 cm, around a pencil. When the pencil is taken out, the paper strip will curl. This is repeated several times. Children then glue these curls around the edge of the bag (fig. 7).

fig. 7

## Animal Parade Place Cards

These can be made by the children and then used as place cards at the table and for Game 3.

**Materials:**
Animal tracer (fig. 23)
Colored construction paper, one sheet per child
Felt pens, crayons, pencils, sequins
Scissors
Glue
1 ball of wool

**Directions:**
1. Fold a piece of colored construction paper in half, large enough to fit animal tracer (fig. 23).
2. Have children trace around the animal and cut it out.
3. Using felt pens, crayons, wool and sequins, children can add various features to make their favorite circus animals.
4. With felt pen, you or the child can print the child's name on the front of the animal (fig. 8).
5. The finished animal can stand by the child's place at the table.

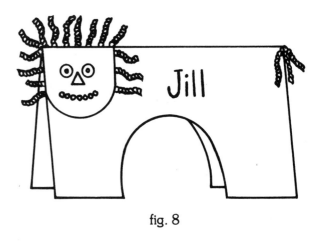

fig. 8

## Clown Face Cookies

Before the party, make your favorite roll-out cookie dough. Cut into circles, bake and cool. Store in an airtight container. At the party, children can ice with white icing. The cookies can be decorated as clown faces with chocolate chips, raisins, peanuts, coconut or cinnamon hearts.

## Elephant Fridge Magnets

Cute as can be!

**Materials:**
$\frac{1}{2}$ walnut shell per child (this will be the
   elephant's body)
Craft clay
Magnetic strip (available in stationery stores)
Glue

**Directions:**
**1.** Make craft clay before the party.

   **Craft Clay**
   125 mL ($\frac{1}{2}$ cup) cornstarch
   250 mL (1 cup) baking soda
   180 mL ($\frac{3}{4}$ cup) water

Combine ingredients and cook until thickened to
dough-like consistency. Turn mixture out onto
pastry board and knead. Keep in plastic bag until
party time.
**2.** Each child takes one walnut shell half and a
ball of craft clay the size of a golf ball.
**3.** Children form four legs and a head out of the
clay. They then attach these to the walnut shell by
pressing the dough to the back edge of the shell. If
necessary, glue on when dry.
**4.** Ears and a trunk can be formed and pressed
onto the head. Pinch dough to form two eyes
(fig. 9).
**5.** Glue a small square of the magnetic strip
onto the inside back of the shell.

fig. 9

## Special Activity

As a special treat for your Circus Celebration, you
can hire a clown to entertain the children. Clowns
are available in most cities (listed in the yellow
pages of the phone book) and will usually per-
form for 30 to 45 minutes.

If you do not wish to hire a clown, have some-
one you know dress up as one instead. The
clown can carry a surprise sack containing some
of your store-bought favors and hand them out to
the children. The clown can also be the storyteller
and read aloud one of the circus books.

Professional or amateur, the clown is sure to be
a hit!

fig. 10

## *Party Schedule*

Be flexible with the time allowed for each activity, as the time for each will vary with the age of the children. If a clown is coming to the party to entertain the children, you will have to consider carefully the time you will be able to spend making favors and playing games. Plan your party to best suit your needs and the interests of the children.

| | | |
|---|---|---|
| Arrival | 10-15 minutes | Children can make their Clown Hat Loot Bags or look at a variety of circus books. |
| Favor activity | 10-15 minutes | Choose from any of the favor activities. If you are making the Elephant Fridge Magnets, do so now. This gives the craft clay a chance to dry. |
| Story | 10 minutes | To set the theme of the Circus Celebration, select a story from the suggested list and you or the clown can read it to the children. |
| Special activity Circus clown performance | 30-45 minutes | The clown can entertain the children during this period. When the performance ends, the birthday child can open the gifts. |
| Game 1 | 5-10 minutes | Clown Toss |
| Favor activity | 10-15 minutes | Choose from any of the favor activities. If you are making the Animal Parade Place Cards, do so now. They can be put at the children's places at the table. |
| Birthday lunch/snack | 15-20 minutes | |
| Favor activity | 10-15 minutes | Choose from any of the remaining favors. If you are face painting, do it last, so the make-up does not have a chance to smear. |
| Game 2 and Game 3 | 15-20 minutes | Who has the Clown? Animal Parade |
| Opening of gifts | 15-20 minutes | |
| Free Play | | |
| Distribution of Clown Hat Loot Bags | | |
| Departure of guests | | |

## *Games*

### *Game 1: Clown Toss*

Draw a clown face on a large sheet of cardboard. Cut out holes where the nose and eyes should be. Make them rather large so the children will be able to throw a bean bag or small foam ball through them without too much difficulty.

Hang the clown face from the ceiling with string. It should be low enough to be at eye-level for the children.

Each child takes a turn throwing three bean bags or foam balls through the holes.

### Game 2: Who has the Clown?

Children sit in a circle on the floor. One person is chosen to be "It." "It" sits on a chair in the middle of the circle. Under the chair, put a clown candle or other small clown of some kind (you can substitute any circus animal for the clown).

"It" has eyes closed or is blindfolded. You or the birthday child walk around the circle and tap a child on the shoulder. This child very quietly takes the clown from under the chair and returns with it to the original spot in the circle. All the children in the circle put their hands behind their backs. "It" opens his or her eyes and has three guesses as to who has the clown. The person who has the clown then becomes "It." The game continues until everyone has had a chance to be "It."

### Game 3: Animal Parade

At the end of every circus there is always a parade. You will need the Animal Parade Place Cards to play this game.

Form a parade line using the Animal Parade Place Cards. The children then sit in a circle around them. Upon a signal, all the children close their eyes and put their heads down. You or the birthday child quietly take one of the circus animals away. When the children lift their heads and open their eyes, they must guess which animal is missing from the parade.

## Suggested Books

The following books are available in local bookstores and public libraries.

|  |  | Age Group |
| --- | --- | --- |
| Banberry, Fred | *Paddington At The Circus* | 4-7 |
| Brun, Helen | *Anna's Circus* | 5-8 |
| Credle, Ellis | *Andy and The Circus* | 5-8 |
| Dubois, William Pené | *The Alligator Case* | 5-8 |
|  | *The Horse In the Camel Suit* | 5-8 |
| Flack, Marjorie | *Wait for William* | 4-6 |
| Freeman, Don | *Bearymore* | 4-6 |
| Gallico, Paul | *The Day Jean-Pierre Joined The Circus* | 6-8 |
| Garbutt, Bernard | *Up Goes The Big Top* | 8 |
| Hill, Eric | *Spot Goes To The Circus* | 3-5 |
| Hoff, Syd | *Henrietta, Circus Star* | 5-8 |
|  | *Ida, The Bareback Rider* | 5-8 |
|  | *Sammy the Seal* | 4-7 |
| Peet, Bill | *Pamela Camel* | 6-8 |
| Peppe, Rodney | *Circus Numbers* | 3-4 |
| Petersham, Maud and Miska | *The Circus Baby* | 4-7 |
| Rey, Margaret and H.A. | *Curious George Goes To The Circus* | 4-6 |
| Schenk De Regniers, Beatrice | *Circus* | 5-8 |

## Party Menu

Pick and choose from these suggestions for your Circus Celebration.

### Animal Bites

Spread peanut butter or processed cheese spread onto slightly frozen bread slices. Press animal-shaped cookie cutters into the bread. Remove the shape you made. Decorate with raisins.

### Frosted Circus Friends

Spread cream cheese on the body of animal crackers. Decorate with coconut or cake sprinkles.

### Elephant Shake

Blend 15 mL (1 tsp.) honey, 15 mL (1 tsp.) peanut butter and 250 mL (1 cup) milk. This makes one serving of a very delicious drink.

### Peanut Butter Balloons

Mix 250 mL (1 cup) peanut butter and 250 mL (1 cup) icing sugar. Stir in 250 mL (1 cup) crispy rice cereal. Roll into round balloon shape. Roll balloons into 125 mL ($1/2$ cup) graham cracker crumbs. Stick pretzel or a piece of shoestring licorice into balloon for the string.

### Clown Cones

Put a scoop of ice cream on each plate. Top with a pointed cone (clown hat). Decorate ice cream with candies, raisins, peanuts or icing. Use icing or canned whipping cream for hair. Make ahead of time and freeze (fig. 11).

fig. 11

### Lion Cake

Using your favorite cake recipe or a commercial cake mix, bake a large round cake and a small round cake. Cool. Cut large cake in half. Separate halves of cake $1\frac{1}{2}''$ at bottom. Place small round cake on top of large split cake, according to fig. 13. Ice and decorate according to fig. 14.

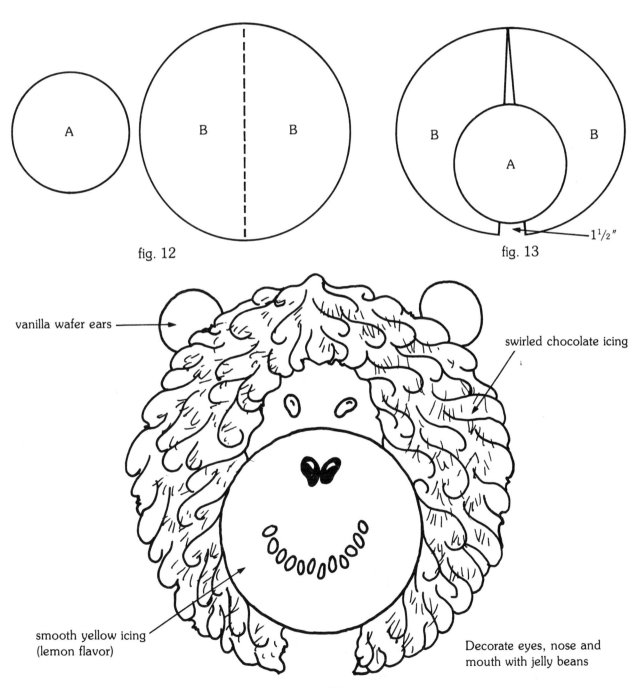

fig. 12

fig. 13

vanilla wafer ears

swirled chocolate icing

smooth yellow icing
(lemon flavor)

Decorate eyes, nose and
mouth with jelly beans

fig. 14

## *Thank-You Notes*

Including a thank-you note in the birthday party plans is an ideal way for your child to show appreciation to the guests.

You may want to include the thank-you note in the guest's Clown Hat Loot Bags, or mail it after the party. By using the clown hat tracer (fig. 24), you can create a special thank-you note that contains a simple message.

Your child can trace and cut the thank-you notes from colored construction paper. These can be decorated with colored stickers, felt pens, crayons, glitter and sequins, if your child wishes. You or your child can print the thank-you message on the hat. Your child can then sign the card (fig. 15).

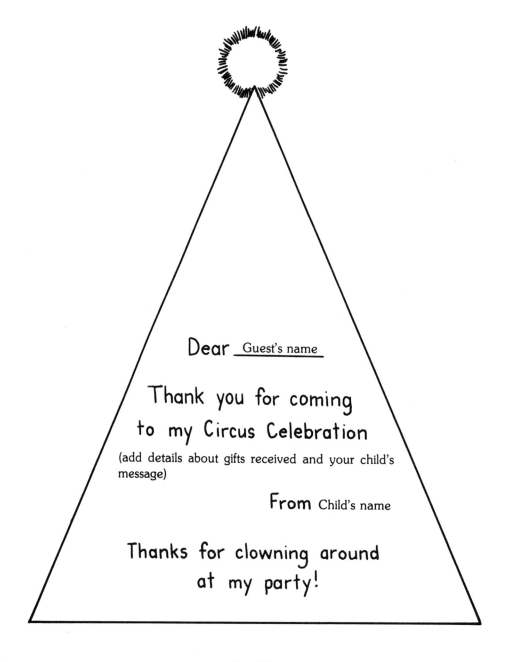

Dear _Guest's name_

Thank you for coming
to my Circus Celebration

(add details about gifts received and your child's message)

From Child's name

Thanks for clowning around
at my party!

fig. 15

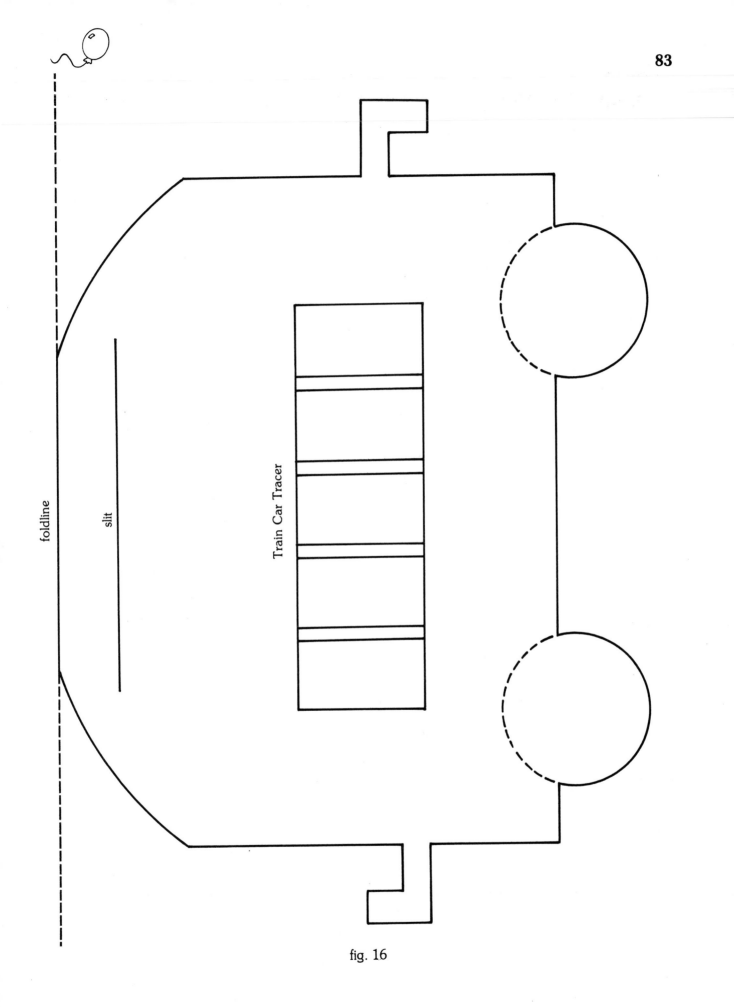

83

foldline

slit

Train Car Tracer

fig. 16

fig. 17

fig. 18

Lion Tracer

Giraffe Tracer

fig. 19

Bear Tracer

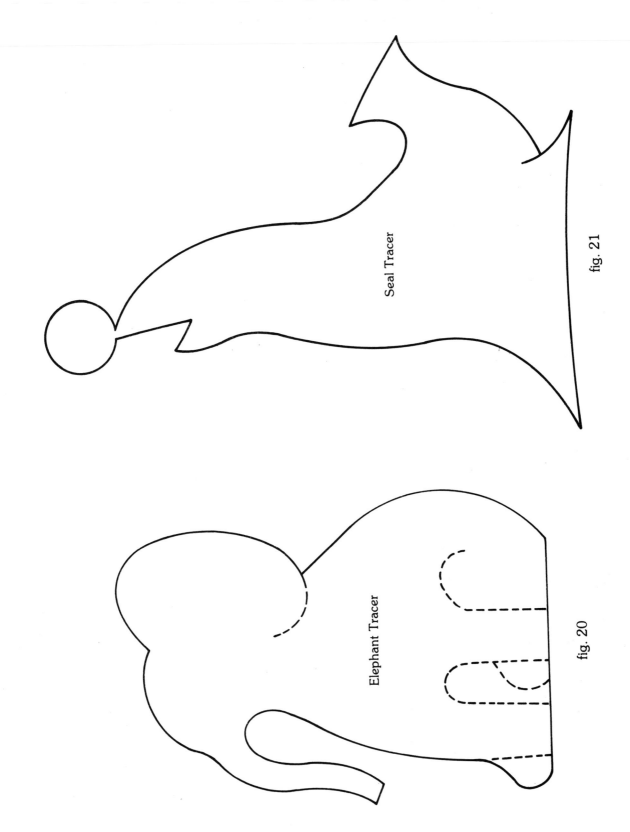

Seal Tracer

fig. 21

Elephant Tracer

fig. 20

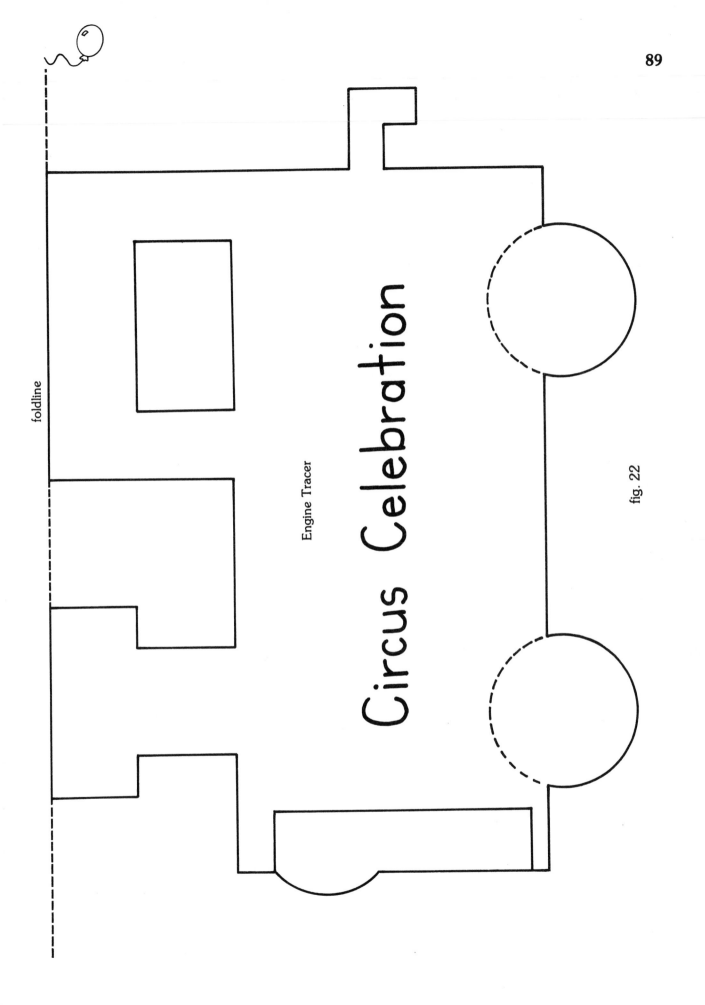

foldline

Engine Tracer

Circus Celebration

fig. 22

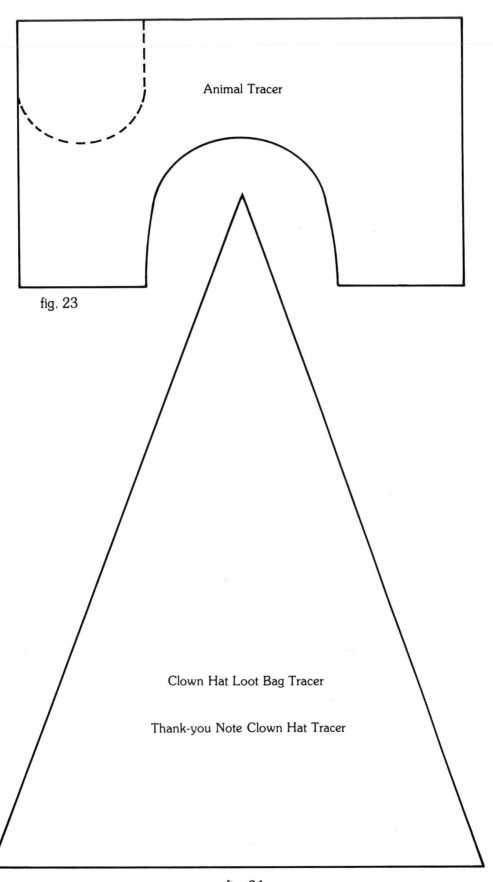

Animal Tracer

fig. 23

Clown Hat Loot Bag Tracer

Thank-you Note Clown Hat Tracer

fig. 24

# A Mouse Tale

*"This one's mice and easy"*

# A Mouse Tale

What's cute and furry and captivates young children's imagination? Mice, mice, mice! Mice are big celebrities in television, movies and storybooks. Let them come to life at your child's birthday party.

Lots of fun-filled mice activities are included in this theme. Watch your guests sprout ears, whiskers and a tail and nibble up the mouse munchies.

With this party, you can have your cheese and eat it too!

## Invitations

Is there anything a mouse likes better than cheese? You and your child can create your own cheese invitations, by following the directions below. Bring your party guests scurrying!

**Materials:**
1 piece of orange construction paper 17 cm ×
    22 cm per child
Scissors
Felt pens

**Directions:**
1.   Fold orange construction paper in half. Place the Cheese Invitation Tracer (fig. 16) on the foldline and trace the pattern.
2.   Cut out the traced cheese, cutting through both pieces of construction paper at the same time.
3.   Do not cut across the top of the cheese sitting on the foldline (fig. 2).
4.   Cut holes out around edge of both pieces (fig. 1). Draw on additional holes with felt pens.
5.   Print the all-important party details inside in bold letters (fig. 3).
6.   Distribute the invitations a week to 10 days before the party—slightly earlier if mailing.

## Decorations

To simulate the sensation of creeping into a mouse hole, cover the doorway leading to the party area with black material or garbage bags.

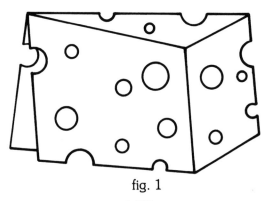

fig. 1

foldline
do not cut here

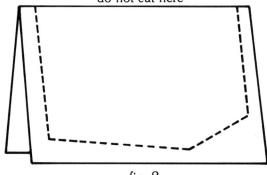

fig. 2

Please come to my Mouse Birthday party
NAME _____
DATE _____
TIME _____
PLACE _____
R.S.V.P. _____

We'll have a <u>hole</u> lot of fun!

fig. 3

Braid three equal lenghts of brown streamers, securing the bottom with a colorful ribbon to create a mouse tail. Attach a tail to each chair at the party table. Finish making the chairs "mice-like" by tying a mouse-shaped balloon, or a balloon with a mouse face drawn on it, to the top of each chair with a long string. Orange material or garbage bags may be used to cover the table and make it look like a piece of cheese. A large stuffed or plastic mouse can be used as a table centerpiece.

# Party Favors

In consultation with your child, decide which party favors you will buy and which you will make.

*Party Favors You Can Buy:*

Mouse erasers
Small packages of cheese and crackers
Mouse-shaped balloons
Mouse books (see Suggested Books list, later in this section)
Mouse cookie cutters
Mouse stickers
Mouse barrettes
Small stuffed mouse

*Party Favors You Can Make:*

Be sure to have the children print their names on whatever they make. As part of the party activities, the children will enjoy making themselves into "mice." The first three favor activities show how.

## Mouse Ears

Easy to make, these will help everyone get in the mood.

**Materials:**
1 piece of heavy construction paper 45 cm × 7.5 cm per child
1 mouse ear tracer per child (fig. 17)
1 piece of heavy construction paper 22 cm × 11 cm per child
Pencils
Glue
Stapler, staples
Scissors

**Directions:**
1.   Give each child a mouse ear tracer (fig. 17), a piece of heavy construction paper (22 cm × 14 cm) and a pencil.
2.   Using the mouse ear tracer, children can trace and cut out two mouse ears.
3.   Glue the two ears on the piece of long construction paper (45 cm × 7.5 cm).
4.   With the help of an adult, children staple the two ends of the long construction paper to make hats that fit their heads (fig. 4). Extra construction paper may have to be cut off.

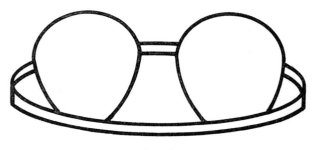

fig. 4

## Mouse Face Make-Up

To complete the transformation of each guest into a mouse, apply make-up to give the child a mouse face. You can use commercial face make-up or make your own, using the following recipe. As the children are busy making their mouse ears and tails, take them aside one at a time to make up their faces.

   * Be sure to check with parents in case any child has allergies to either type of make-up.

### Face Make-Up
1 pen
2 parts vegetable shortening
1 part cornstarch
Color with powdered tempera paint.
Use fingertips to apply.
Removes easily!

## Mouse Tails

No mouse is complete without a tail!

### Materials:
1 round piece of black felt per child, 16 cm in
    diameter
1 safety pin per child
Scissors

### Directions:
**1.** Give each child a round piece of black felt
and a pair of scissors.
**2.** Have each child cut a piece of felt in a
diminishing spiral pattern to form the Mouse Tail.
To make this easier, you may choose to draw the
spiral beforehand on each piece of felt, using
white chalk (fig. 5).
**3.** Attach the Mouse Tail to each guest's lower
back with a small safety pin (fig. 6).

## Mouse Bookmarks

### Materials:
1 piece of felt 5 cm × 5 cm per child, any color
1 piece of felt 1.5 cm × 18 cm per child, any
    color
1 mouse body tracer per child (fig. 18)
Scissors
White glue
Pens
Sequins

### Directions:
**1.** Give each child one piece of felt (5 cm ×
5 cm), a pen and a mouse body tracer.
**2.** Have each child trace and cut out a mouse
body.
**3.** Using leftover scraps, have the children cut
and glue on two ears, a small nose and whiskers.
They may wish to trade scraps with another guest
in order to have a different color of felt to use for
these features.
**4.** Glue on two sequins for eyes.
**5.** Glue on a long piece of felt (1.5 cm ×
18 cm) for the tail (fig. 7).

diminishing
spiral pattern
fig. 5

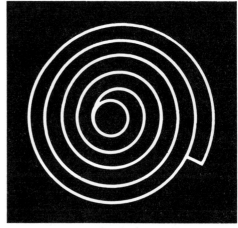

cut tail
fig. 6

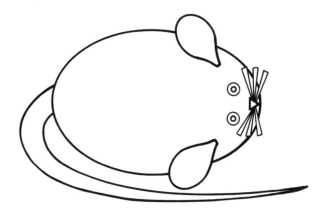

fig. 7

## Mouse Bag Puppet (Loot Bag)

Not only are these fun to play with, but they are also great to carry party favors home in.

**Materials:**
1 brown paper lunch bag per child
Felt pens, crayons
White glue
Scissors
Masking tape
1 piece colored construction paper per child
   22 cm × 14 cm
1 piece of wool per child, 20 cm long

**Directions:**
**1.** Give each child a brown paper lunch bag.
**2.** Children can decorate the bottom half of the bag, using felt pens and construction paper, to

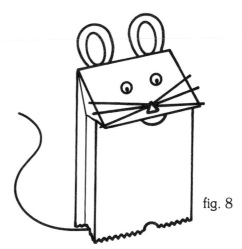

fig. 8

make the face of a mouse. Ears can also be glued on.
**3.** A piece of wool taped inside the open end of the bag will create a mouse tail (fig. 8) .

## Mouse Pretzels

Make these in advance for a party favor for the children to take home or eat as part of the birthday lunch/snack. Alternatively, prepare the dough ahead of time and have the children form the mouse-shaped pretzels.

**Pretzel Recipe**
375 mL (1½ cups) all-purpose flour
160 mL (⅔ cup) milk
125 mL (½ cup) shredded cheddar cheese
30 mL (2 tbsp.) soft butter
10 mL (2 tsp.) baking powder
5 mL (1 tsp.) sugar
5 mL (1 tsp.) salt
1 egg
salt (coarse, fine, seasoned or
an herb substitute)

**Directions:**
**1.** Mix flour, baking powder, sugar and salt with cheese, butter, and then milk to form a soft dough.
**2.** Form into a ball and knead a few times until smooth.
**3.** Divide dough into quarters, then cut into 16 pieces. Roll each piece into a snake approximately 30 cm (12″) long (fig. 9).
**4.** Form the snake into a mouse shape by taking 20 cm (8″) of the snake and curving it back on top of itself to form the head and body. The remaining 10 cm (4″) forms the tail (fig. 10).
**5.** Brush with beaten egg and sprinkle with salt.
**6.** Bake at 200°C (400°F) for 20-25 minutes. Makes 16 Mouse Pretzels.

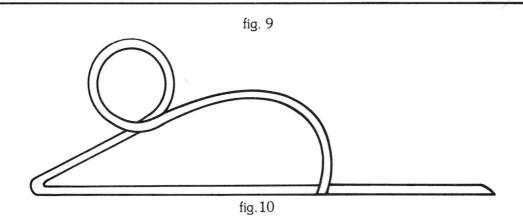

fig. 9

fig.10

## *Party Schedule*

The following is a suggested schedule for planning your party. Be flexible with the time allowed for each activity, taking into consideration the age and interests of the children.

| | | |
|---|---|---|
| Arrival | 10-15 minutes | Children can begin making Mouse Ears and Mouse Tails. Doing these early will help everyone get into the mood of the party. As well, the children will enjoy impersonating mice when playing the games. |
| Story | 10 minutes | Choose a story from the suggested list to help establish the theme of the party. |
| Favor activities | 15-20 minutes | Complete Mouse Ears and Mouse Tails, Mouse Face Make-Up, Mouse Pretzels. If you plan to have the children make and eat these as part of the birthday lunch/ snack, start them now. |
| Game 1 | 10 minutes | Cat and Mouse |
| Game 2 | 10 minutes | Mousetrap |
| Favor activities | 15 minutes | Mouse Bag Puppets (Loot Bag), Mouse Bookmark |
| Birthday lunch/snack | 20 minutes | |
| Game 3 | 10 minutes | Squeak, Squeak |
| Opening of gifts | 15-20 minutes | |
| Free play | | |
| Distribution of Mouse Bag Puppets (Loot Bags) | | |
| Departure of guests | | |

# Games

## Game 1: Cat and Mouse

This is an active game that is best played in a large area. Have all the children except two join hands to form a circle. Then have them drop hands and take two big steps backwards. This will ensure there is enough room between the children to play the game. Designate one of the two children outside the circle to be the "cat" and the other to be the "mouse." Have the "mouse" stand in the middle of the circle and the "cat" on the outside of the circle. When you say "go," the "cat" chases the "mouse" in, out, and around the circle, attempting to tag. When the "cat" touches the "mouse," the "cat" comes into the center of the circle and becomes the new "mouse". The former "mouse" joins the children standing in the circle and a new "cat" is chosen. Continue playing until each child has had a chance to be both the "cat" and the "mouse."

## Game 2: Mousetrap

Divide the children into two groups. Have one group join hands to form a circle, while the second group stands outside of the circle. Tell the children holding hands that they are a "mousetrap" and the children outside the circle are the "mice." When the command "mousetrap open" is given, the children in the circle lift their joined hands high in the air. The "mice" then run in and out of the circle by going underneath their arms. When the command "mousetrap closed" is given, the children in the circle quickly bring their hands down. Any "mice" in the circle have been caught in the "mousetrap" and become part of the circle. Continue in this manner until all the "mice" have been caught. Then have all the children who have been "mice" form a circle to be the new "mousetrap," while the other children become the "mice."

## Game 3: Squeak, Squeak

Ask all the children to sit in a circle. Choose one child to stand in the center of the circle and be blindfolded. Tell the children you are going to point to one child in the circle to say "squeak, squeak" like a mouse. That child's voice should be disguised to make it difficult for the person in the center of the circle to guess the "mouse." Explain that the other children must sit very quietly and not make a sound. Then point to the child who is to squeak. Remove the blindfold from the child in the center of the circle, who should then make a guess on who is the "mouse." Offer three guesses. (It is important to stress to the other children that they do not give any clues as to who said "squeak, squeak.") When the child guesses correctly, he or she joins the other children in the circle and the "mouse" comes to the center of the circle to be blindfolded. Continue the game until everyone has had a chance to be the "mouse" and be blindfolded.

# Suggested Books

All of these books are available in local bookstores and libraries.

| | | Age Group |
|---|---|---|
| Aesop's Fables | *The Country Mouse and the Town Mouse* | 5-8 |
| Brandenberg, Franz | *It's Not My Fault* | 6-8 |
| | *Nice New Neighbors* | 6-8 |
| Durrell, Julie | *Mouse Tails* | 3-6 |
| Freeman, Don | *The Guard Mouse* | 7-8 |
| Gordon, Margaret | *The Supermarket Mice* | 4-6 |
| Kraus, Robert | *Another Mouse to Feed* | 3-5 |
| | *Whose Mouse Are You?* | 3-5 |
| Lionni, Leo | *Alexander and the Wind-Up Mouse* | 6-8 |
| | *Frederick* | 6-8 |
| | *Theodore and the Talking Mushroom* | 6-8 |
| Lobel, Arnold | *Mouse Soup* | 5-8 |
| | *Mouse Tales* | 5-8 |
| Miller, Edna | *Mousekin's Golden House* | 6-8 |
| | *Mousekin's Family* | 6-8 |
| | *Mousekin Finds A Friend* | 6-8 |
| Numeroff, Laura | *If You Give a Mouse a Cookie* | 4-6 |
| Raskin, Ellen | *Moose, Goose, and Little Nobody* | 4-5 |
| Roche, Patricia | *Webster and Arnold and the Giant Box* | 6-8 |
| Szekeres, Cindy | *Counting Book* | 3-4 |
| Waber, Bernard | *Mice on My Mind* | 6-8 |
| Wells, Rosemary | *Stanley and Rhoda* | 4-6 |

# Party Menu

Select a few of the following "mouse munchies" for your child's party. Discuss the menu with your child so that favorite foods are included. Prepare the snacks and birthday cake shortly before the party.

### Mouseshake

Prepare plenty of your child's favorite flavor of milkshake.

### Mouse Fruit Salad

Place half of a canned pear on a bed of lettuce. This forms the body of the mouse. Using colored plastic toothpicks, stick in: two pitted prunes for ears, two raisins for the eyes; and half of a glazed cherry for the nose. Make thin carrot curls to place beside the pear as the whiskers and tail.

### Cheese and Crackers

Put out a tray of your child's favorites for the little mice to nibble on while waiting for the main course.

### Macaroni And Cheese

An old favorite! Prepare your own recipe or buy a heat-and-serve or frozen brand.

## Fun and Furry Mouse Cakes

Bake your child's favorite cake in two 22 cm (9″) round cake pans. Also bake four cupcakes. Spread icing or jam on the top of one layer, then place the second layer on top of it. Cut the combined two layers in half and separate (fig. 12).

Ice cakes and cupcakes according to fig. 13 and assemble. Then decorate using suggested candies.

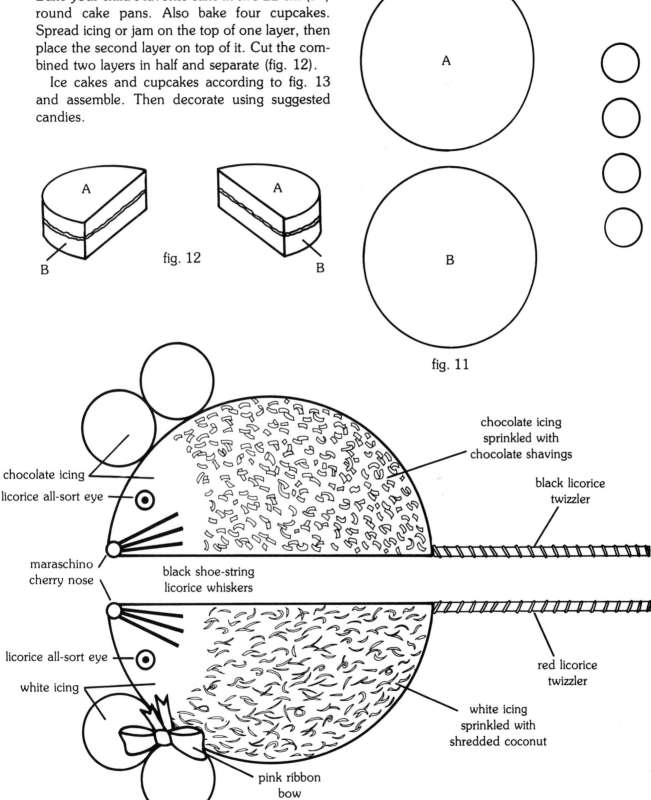

fig. 12

fig. 11

chocolate icing sprinkled with chocolate shavings

black licorice twizzler

chocolate icing

licorice all-sort eye

maraschino cherry nose

black shoe-string licorice whiskers

red licorice twizzler

licorice all-sort eye

white icing

white icing sprinkled with shredded coconut

pink ribbon bow

fig. 13

## *Thank-You Notes*

Complete your birthday celebrations by helping your child say thank you to their guests. The Mouse Thank-You Cards are easy to make and may be included in each guest's loot bag or sent out after the party.

Using fig. 19, have your child trace and cut out

the thank-you notes from the colored construction paper. With felt pens, decorate the front of the note (fig. 14). You or your child can print the simple thank-you message on the back of the card (fig. 15). Then your child can sign it.

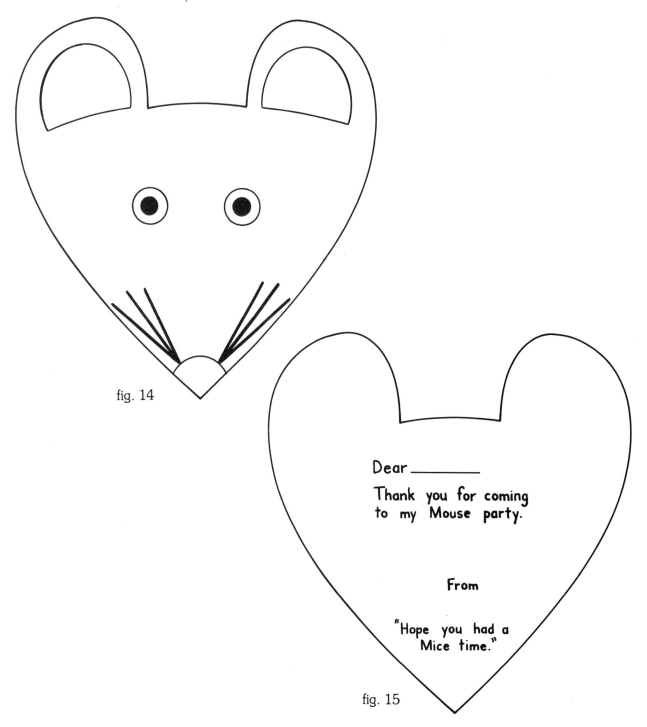

fig. 14

Dear _____
Thank you for coming to my Mouse party.

From

"Hope you had a Mice time."

fig. 15

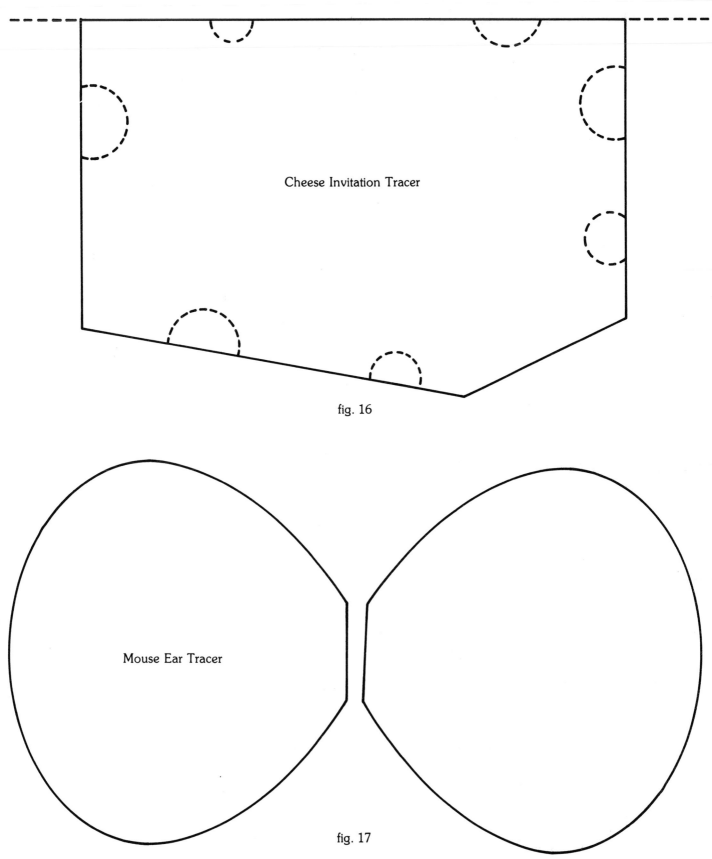

Cheese Invitation Tracer

fig. 16

Mouse Ear Tracer

fig. 17

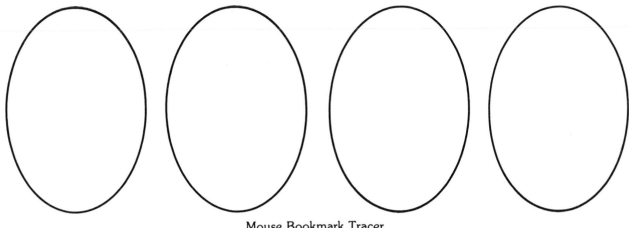

Mouse Bookmark Tracer
fig. 18

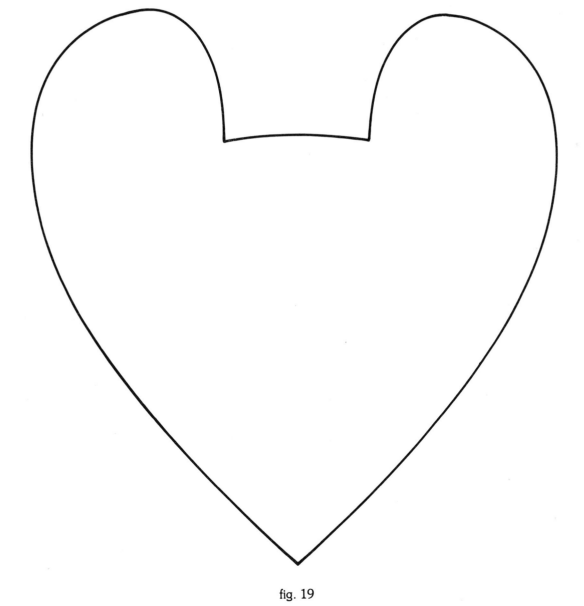

fig. 19

# Under
# the Sea

You'll have a whale of a time!

# Under the Sea

Got a party to plan? Got that sinking feeling?

You can go overboard and still stay afloat with this "under-the-sea" celebration.

The children will meet under-the-sea creatures, go on a deep-sea hunt and find a buried treasure. They'll head home with a netful of memories.

Buoy, this one's easy!

## Invitations

You and your child can begin your Under the Sea Birthday Party by making these fishbowl invitations.

### Materials:
Blue construction paper
Orange construction paper
Fishbowl tracer (fig. 13)
Goldfish tracer (fig. 14)
Crayons, felt pens, pencil
Scissors
Buttons
Sequins
Glue
1 ball of wool

### Directions:
1. Fold blue construction paper in half to fit fishbowl tracer (fig. 13). Place tracer on the foldline and trace around pattern. Cut out traced fishbowl, cutting through both pieces of construction paper at the same time. Do not cut across the top of the bowl on the foldline (fig. 2).
2. Place goldfish tracer (fig. 14) on orange construction paper. Trace and cut out. Glue fish on front of fishbowl invitation.
3. Decorate invitation by gluing a button eye and a wool mouth on the fish. Add wool and sequins to represent plant life and soil in the bottom of the bowl.

fig. 1

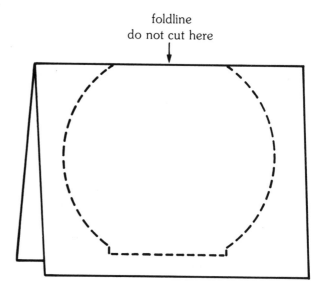

foldline
do not cut here

fig. 2

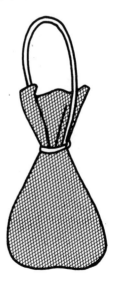

Join us for a birthday splash!

NAME _____

DATE _____

TIME _____

PLACE _____

R.S.V.P. _____

Come make waves at my party!

fig. 3

**4.** Print in bold letters, inside the invitation, all the important party details (fig. 3).

**5.** Distribute your invitations a week to 10 days before the party—slightly earlier if mailing.

# Decorations

The party room can be gaily decorated to represent your "Under the Sea" theme. Green, brown and blue streamers hung from the ceiling can masquerade as seaweed and water. Using the fish tracer (fig. 15), cut out several fish. These can be decorated using felt pens and crayons and then hung about the room.

If there are pet fish or other marine life in the home, use them as a centerpiece, placing the bowl or aquarium on the table. If no marine life is available, fill a clear bowl with water and add blue food coloring. Plastic fish, snakes, turtles, seahorses and starfish will make a great imaginary aquarium.

Section off a corner or part of the room by hanging large clear sheets of plastic from the ceiling (available at any hardware store). Behind it, place flippers, goggles, snorkels, fishing rods and stuffed creatures. The children will enjoy playing in this "fish bowl."

# Party Favors

When planning your birthday celebration, choose the favors you would like to make from the selection below. Be sure to consult your child in this decision. Children will enjoy carrying their party favors home in their Fish Net Loot Bags. Included also is a list of party favors you can buy.

You may decide to make some of the party favors ahead of time, depending on the age of the children and the length of the party.

*Party Favors You Can Buy:*

Plastic marine life (fish, seals, turtles, snakes, starfish, crocodiles, crabs, whales, etc.)
Seashells, real or plastic
Bubbles
Cookie cutters (fish, whales, etc.)
Miniature plastic divers
Goggles
Plastic boats
Dissolving capsules forming sea creatures (available in toystores, novelty shops)
Seashell soap
Nautical books
Stickers

*Party Favors You Can Make:*

## Fish Nets (Loot Bags)

You may choose to make these just before the children go home, so they can wrap up all their party favors.

An alternative to making these fish net loot bags is to save the net bags in which onions are packed and use them instead.

fig. 4

**Materials:**

Garden/Fish net, (available at hardware and gardening stores) or veil netting, one piece per child 36 cm × 36 cm

String or ribbon, 20 cm per child

**Directions:**

**1.** Ask the guests to gather their party favors and place them in the center of their nets.

**2.** Take the four corners and tie a knot, using string or ribbon.

**3.** Tie the two ends of the string together, so the children may wear the bags home over their wrists.

## Deep Sea Hunt

Make these early in the party so they have time to bake and cool. The playdough should be prepared before the party.

**Materials:**

1 batch of Baker's Playdough (see recipe below)

Wax paper

Toothpicks

Pipe cleaners, two per child

1 plastic tomato basket per child

Pictures of marine life

Marine life cookie cutters (optional—available in kitchen specialty shops)

**Baker's Playdough**

500 mL (2 cups) flour

250 mL (1 cup) salt

250 mL (1 cup) water

Knead until smooth. Place in bowl and cover with plastic wrap until needed.

**Directions:**

**1.** Give each child a piece of wax paper to work

on, and a ball of playdough about the size of a large apple.

**2.** The children can mold their playdough to make fish, seahorses, whales or other marine life, using your pictures and their imaginations to guide them. They may also roll their playdough out and use cookie cutters (fish, stars) to cut out their animals.

**3.** Place the completed marine life on a cookie sheet and bake in the oven at 120°C (250°F) for 40 minutes.

**4.** After allowing the marine life to cool, place them in the fish traps (tomato baskets) to take home.

**5.** Pipe cleaners can be attached at both ends to form handles for the fish trap (fig. 5).

## Deep-Sea Diving Goggles

These are easy to make, but children may require help cutting the eyes out.

**Materials:**

1 piece of construction paper (any color) per child, to fit goggles tracer

Goggles tracer (fig. 16)

2 pipe cleaners per child

Stapler, staples

Pencil, crayons, felt pens

**Directions:**

**1.** Children can trace and cut out goggles from tracer (fig. 16)

**2.** Cut out eyeholes as shown on tracer.

**3.** The diving goggles can be decorated with felt pens and crayons. Print name on inside.

**4.** Staple a pipe cleaner at each end and bend to fit around the child's ears (fig. 6).

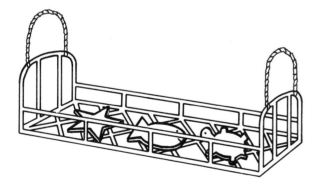

fig. 5

fig. 6

## Fishing Boats

Very easy! Have ready a sink or bowl filled with water so the children can float their boats when finished.

**Materials:**
1/2 walnut shell per child
Plasticine
Toothpicks
Small pieces of construction paper, any color
Scissors
Felt pens, crayons
Glue

**Directions:**
1. Give each child a walnut shell half.
2. Have each child firmly push a small piece of plasticine into bottom of shell.
3. Children can cut out small rectangles or triangles from paper and decorate them as the masts.
4. Ask the party guests to poke toothpicks through the masts or glue masts to the toothpicks.
5. The toothpicks can then be stuck into the plasticine (fig. 7).
6. Set the boats in the water.

## Marine Life Mobile

Copy marine life tracers (figs. 17-20) on to stiff cardboard and cut out ahead of time, to make it easier for the children to trace.

**Materials:**
Colored construction paper
Marine life tracers (figs. 17, 18, 19, & 20)
1 hanger per child
Scissors
Single-hole punch
String
Crayons, felt pens, pencils

**Directions:**
1. Have each child pick and trace two or three marine life creatures (figs. 17-20).
2. Children may then cut out and decorate their creatures with crayons and felt pens.
3. Punch a hole in the top of each one and attach to hanger with string (about 30 cm long) (fig. 8).
4. Hang mobiles around the room until the children are ready to take them home.

fig. 7

fig. 8

## Party Schedule

Here is a suggested party schedule to guide you through your birthday celebration. Be flexible with the time allowed for each activity; consider your guest's ages.

| | | |
|---|---|---|
| Arrival | 10-15 minutes | Have a variety of "Under the Sea" books set out. Children will also enjoy playing in the imaginary "fishbowl" if you decide to set one up. |
| Story | 10 minutes | Choose a story from the suggested list to help set the mood of this "Under the Sea" birthday theme. |
| Favor activities | 15-20 minutes | One or two favors can be made at this time. If you are doing the Deep Sea Hunt, start it now so it will have time to bake and cool. |
| Game 1 | 10 minutes | Buried Treasure |
| Birthday lunch/snack | 20 minutes | |
| Game 2 | 10 minutes | Deep Sea Guess |
| Favor activities | 15-20 minutes | Make one or more of the remaining party favors. Fish Nets should be made last so all other party favors can be tucked into them. |
| Opening of gifts | 15-20 minutes | |
| Free play | | |
| Distribution of Fish Nets (Loot Bags) | | |
| Departure of guests | | |

# Games

### Game 1: Buried Treasure

Hide one party favor per child around the room before you begin this activity.

**Materials:**
String, 30 cm long
Magnet
Paper clips
Pail
1 marine life tracer per child (figs. 17-20)
1 party favor per child

**Directions:**
1. Using one marine life tracer per child, write out simple directions to lead the child to their hidden favor (Example: "Jill, take 10 steps backwards and look under the blue pillow"). Attach a paper clip to each tracer and place in the pail. Attach the string to the magnet.
2. To play the game, children dangle the magnet into the pail until they "catch" their marine life. Help the children read the directions that will lead them to their "buried treasure." Play the game until all the sea life has been caught and each child has a favor.

### Game 2: Deep Sea Guess

This is lots of fun for any age!

**Directions:**
1. Fill a large tub or pail with water and add blue food coloring to make your ocean.

**2.** Drop one plastic marine life creature per child in the pail (large inexpensive assortment available at toy stores).

**3.** Blindfold one child at a time. Each child reaches in and chooses one favor. The child tries to identify the marine life creature before taking the blindfold off.

**4.** Each guest keeps the marine life creature and adds it to his or her loot bag at the end of the party.

## Suggested Books

All of these books are available in local stores and libraries.

|  |  | Age Group |
|---|---|---|
| Asch, Frank | *Just Like Daddy* | 3-6 |
| Barr, Catherine | *Sammy Seal of the Circus* | 5-8 |
| Dodd, Lynley | *The Smallest Turtle* | 4-8 |
| Duvoisin, Roger | *The Christmas Whale* | 3-8 |
| Ipcar, Dahlov | *The Biggest Fish in the Sea* | 5-8 |
| Kalan, Robert | *Jump, Frog, Jump* | 3-5 |
| Kellogg, Steven | *The Mysterious Tadpole* | 5-8 |
| Lionni, Leo | *Cornelius* | 5-8 |
|  | *Fish Is Fish* | 4-8 |
|  | *Swimmy* | 4-8 |
| Palmer, Helen | *A Fish out of Water* | 4-8 |
| Peet, Bill | *Cyrus, the Unsinkable Sea Serpent* | 6-8 |
| Wildsmith, Brian | *Fishes* | 5-8 |
| Zalben, Jan | *Penny and the Captain* | 8 |

## Party Menu

Pick and choose from these divers' delicacies to make a lunch/snack that is sure to delight any group of young divers!

### Banana Boat Sandwiches

Spread peanut butter on one slice of bread. Place a banana half on top and close the ends with pretzels.

### Octopuses

Cook frozen fish patties according to package instructions. For an Octopus, poke eight pretzels into each fish patty to make eight legs.

fig. 9

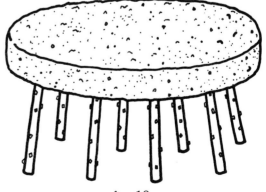

fig. 10

### Jellyfish

Prepare strawberry or raspberry jelly powder according to package instructions. Pour into ice cube trays. Chill in fridge until firm. Turn out onto plates as individual "jellyfish."

### The Frothy Seas

Children will enjoy this foamy drink! Blend one can frozen grape juice concentrate, 250 mL (1 cup) milk and 500 mL (2 cups) vanilla ice cream for 30 seconds. This makes 4 servings.

### Turtle Cake

Using your favorite cake recipe, bake cake in a large round oven-proof bowl and make six cupcakes as well. Assemble, trim round edges off cupcake for neck, ice and decorate as shown (fig. 11).

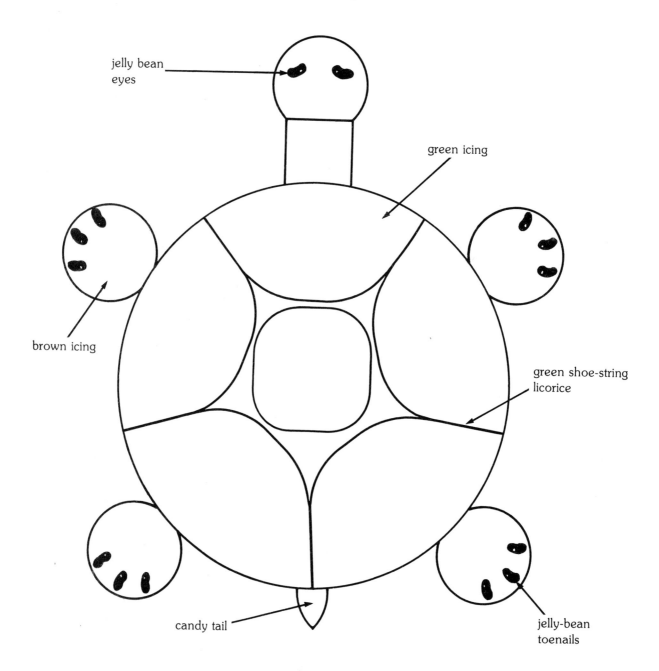

jelly bean eyes

green icing

brown icing

green shoe-string licorice

candy tail

jelly-bean toenails

fig. 11

## Thank-You Notes

Sending thank-you notes to your party guests is an ideal way for your child to say thank you. These may be sent home in the Fish Net Loot Bags or mailed after the party.

By using the fishbowl tracer (fig. 13), you can make your own thank-you notes. Trace and cut them from construction paper. The outside can then be decorated and you or your child can print the thank-you message on the inside. Help your child to sign each card (fig. 12) .

Dear _____

Thank you for coming to my
Under the Sea birthday.

(add details about gifts received and your child's message)

**From** Child's name

"Hope you had a splash!"

fig. 12

foldline

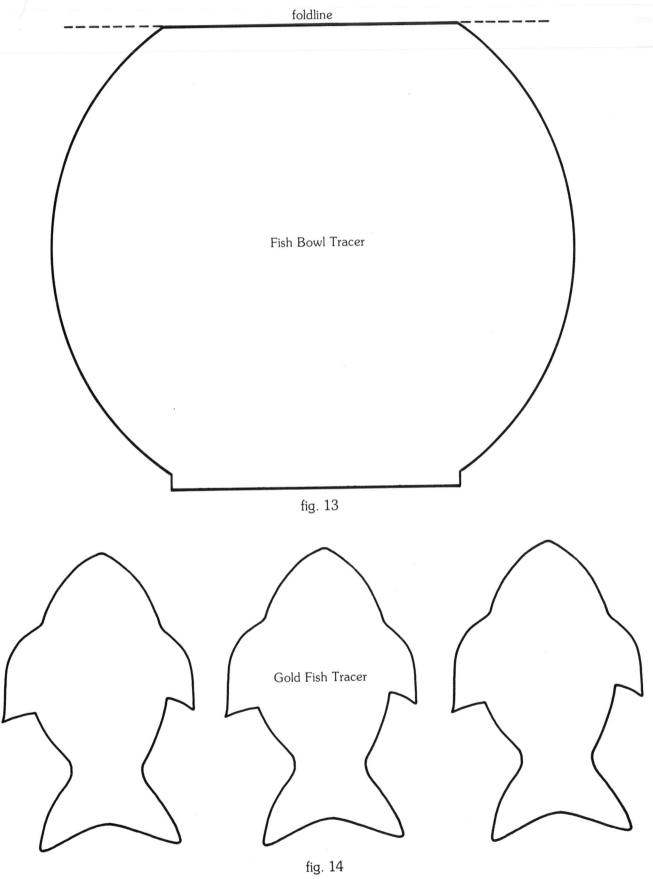

Fish Bowl Tracer

fig. 13

Gold Fish Tracer

fig. 14

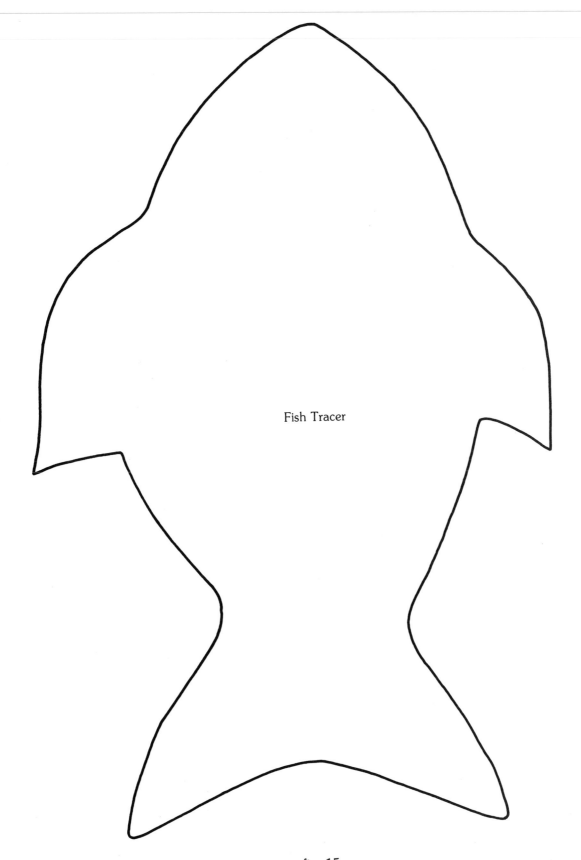

Fish Tracer

fig. 15

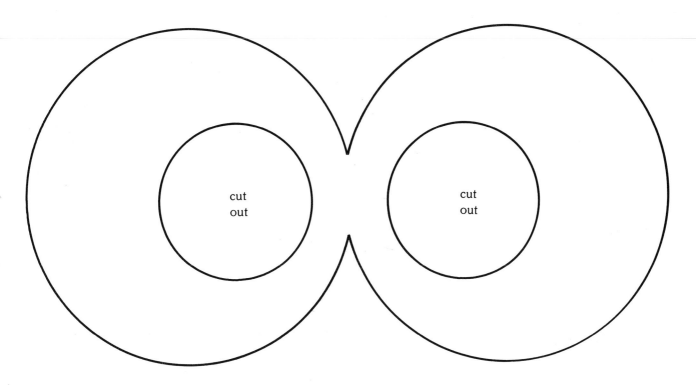

Goggles Tracer

fig. 16

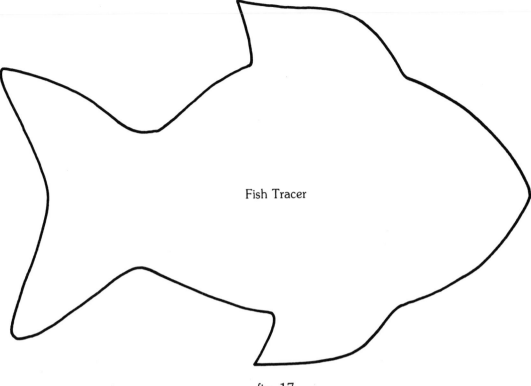

Fish Tracer

fig. 17

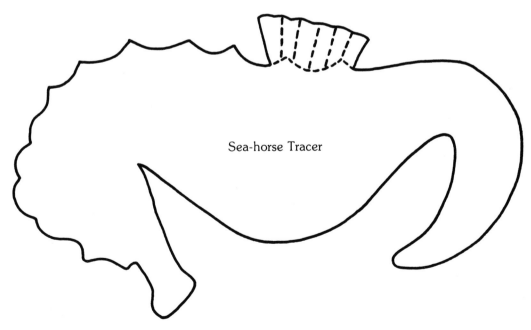

Sea-horse Tracer

fig. 18

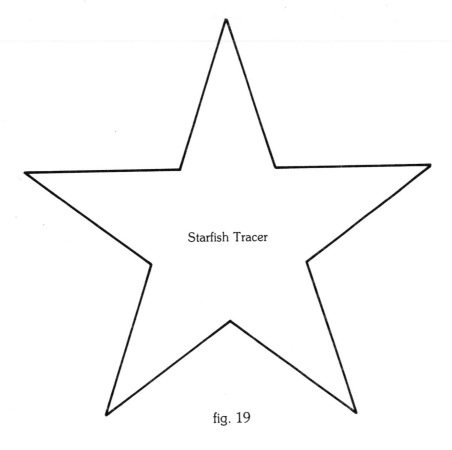

Starfish Tracer

fig. 19

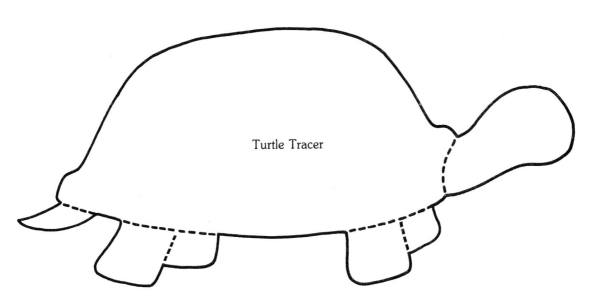

Turtle Tracer

fig. 20